Learn
to Surf

Learn to Surf

James
MacLaren

The Lyons Press

Printed in the United States of America

Designed by Joel Friedlander Publishing Services

All photographs by Mark Grabowski unless otherwise noted.
Illustration on pages 11 by Martha Weston. Illustrations on pages 45 and 46 by Joel Friedlander Publishing Services.

10 9 8 7 6 5 4

Library of Congress Cataloging-in-Publication Data

McLaren, James, 1951–
    Learn to surf / James McLaren.
       p. cm.
    Includes index.
    ISBN 1-55821-568-9
    1. Surfing. I. Title.
    GV840.S8M23   1997
    797.3´2—dc21   97-1394
                                         CIP

Warning! Surf at your own risk!

Any injuries resulting from surfing are the sole responsibility of the individual who willfully and knowingly engages in a sport known and here pronounced to be extremely dangerous. If you surf long enough, you will get injured, regardless of which book you read or what kind of instructions you receive.

Contents

For Lilly and JoAnn, who said "Okay."

Instructions for Reading This Book

First, a few presumptions have been made about you, the reader. One is that you know nothing, or very nearly nothing, about the nuts and bolts of surfing.

Another presumption is that you understand none of the lingo associated with surfing. Do *not* make the grave mistake of thinking that you're familiar with it just because you watched some movie about surfing or heard someone on CNN say "hang ten." In this book I use the bare minimum of lingo and even go so far as to call things by names you'll understand but experienced surfers probably wouldn't. A glossary of surfing terms at the end of the book will clue you in to the real lingo once you've learned the material.

If you know nothing about surfing, don't try to pick up this book and read a little bit, go and try out what you learned, read a little bit more, go out and try that, and so on.

Read it all the way through. *Force* yourself to finish it prior to going surfing.

You might not really understand it all on that first read. Just read it through for content. Understanding will come later.

Introduction: Why Surf?

Why surf? Good question. On the face of things it looks like an awful lot of time and trouble spent in the pursuit of mere seconds of enjoyment. But of course, there's a bit more to it than that. Quite a bit.

Surfing is unique. There's nothing else like it. There you are, astride the crested back of an open-ocean roller, hammering toward the shore, propelled by an elemental force of nature. Deep-sea swells are not trivial things. Throughout history they've inspired well-deserved fear among swimmers, sailors, fishermen, and all the others who've come up against their power. And yet, despite the dreadful aspects of the beast, as a skilled surfer you are its master. You have successfully harnessed the wave's energy and turned it to your own ends. This is heady stuff.

Of course you haven't actually tamed the wave you're riding. You've merely learned to move in harmony with it. Turn your back on a wave, even for an instant, and it'll likely thrash you as you've never been thrashed before.

The element of danger is always present when surfing—this is what makes the sport so exciting. The trick is to keep the danger within manageable limits so that you can drink up the exhilaration and not spend every moment worrying about getting the holy snot pounded out of you.

This little book aims to assist you in your efforts by walking you out into the shallow end, where you can try your luck with baby waves before matching wits with Leviathan in his lair.

What It's Like (and Not Like)

Despite its uniqueness, surfing is not without its parallels in human endeavor. If you've ever watched or done any skateboarding or snowboarding (note the *boarding* in those two words), you'll immediately see that many control movements in those sports bear more than a passing resemblance to the control moves employed by surfers.

This is no accident. In all three sports people are traveling fast and maneuvering a device that they're perched upon with their feet planted crosswise to their direction of travel. For those subtypes of surfing where the rider doesn't stand up, the parallels are different but still exist. Bodyboarding has many similarities with tobogganing. Bodysurfing mimics skydiving, of all things, in many respects. Your familiarity with any of these other sports can be called upon to help you to learn to surf.

But beware. In many important ways, surfing is really like none of the activities just mentioned. The parallels go only so far and not an inch farther. Don't plan on hitting the waves and tearing it up on your first day just because you're an expert-level skateboarder, snowboarder, tobogganer, or skydiver. In surfing parlance, on your first day in the water you're a *kook.* And don't plan on progressing beyond the kook stage overnight. Learning the intricacies of surfing takes *time.* There are no shortcuts. You're going to be training your mind and body in a whole series of reflexes you've never encountered before.

There are also activities that people incorrectly believe to be similar to surfing. The three main ones are snow skiing, waterskiing, and windsurfing (sailboarding). These sports have *nothing* in common with surfing.

Of the three, windsurfing is probably the most deceptive. After all, you're out there on the water, whamming along at a high rate of speed. And you're standing on a board with your feet planted crosswise to your direction of travel. Don't be fooled. Windsurfing is so utterly different from surfing that it actually puts you at a disadvantage when it comes to learning how to surf compared with people who've never windsurfed at all. If you're an experienced windsurfer, time and again your body is going to hand you the wrong reflex when you're learning to surf. You'll have to *unlearn* the windsurfing reflexes in order to learn the surfing reflexes. The same goes for snow and waterskiing.

But don't think that because you're an ace in deep powder snow, you'll crash and burn as a surfer. Not so. Many, many people are adept at both of these sports. So don't worry. You'll be fine. But you'll have to put in the time just like all the rest of us.

The World of Surfing

So, you've decided to have a go at it. You're going to try to learn to surf. Perhaps you ought to have a look at just what it is, exactly, that you're getting yourself into here.

Surfing is a world unto itself. A mysterious parallel dimension filled with wonders, terrors, and whackos, all hiding right out there in plain sight where you can't see any of them. Strange, eh? That, of course, is part of the attraction of the sport.

Whether you know it or not, you're going to be getting up close and personal with a whole panoply of people, things, and situations the likes of which you've never encountered before.

If you've got a media education on surfing, you've got no education on surfing at all. Well . . . not exactly. In fact it's even worse than that. You have less than no education. You have a kind of negative education. The media, through television and movies, has given people a horribly distorted and misleading picture of surfing.

First, surfing is a physically demanding *sport*. There isn't a muscle group in your body that won't get a workout during a surf session. Which is not to say that you've got to be built like Arnold Schwarzenegger in order to surf—not at all. Go have a look at some surfers somewhere. You'll see every healthy body type imaginable.

Second, surfers don't go around saying "dude" or "hang ten" all the time, or even ever. The only people who talk like that are either actors on TV or in a movie, or TV announcers who've been given a surfing-related assignment. If any of these people, or the folks writing for them, had done the least bit of home-work on the sport, they would've known that real surfers don't talk like that.

But surfers don't really care that they're consistently misrep-resented by the media. This is one of the great secret strengths of the sport: Surfers are quite content to let the world lurch madly along just so long as it leaves them alone. Surfing is a very pecu-liar ivory tower in which the initiates get on with the business of doing what they do with a minimal amount of interference from the world at large.

So who are surfers?

The majority are young. An awful lot of people, when their bodies start aging, give the sport up. They can no longer per-form at the level they used to, and the frustrations caused by this drop in performance have caused many an old surfer to hang it up for good. Today, with the resurgence in longboard-ing—which allows older surfers to keep catching and riding waves even when their bodies no longer have the strength, spring, and resiliency of youth—this demographic is changing. But the youngsters are still a majority in the surfing community.

The Wonders

The ocean is a wondrous thing. Here's this great globe-girdling wilderness, and you get to go play in it. What could be better?

On days when the breeze is blowing off the land into the faces of sparkling blue and green waves with white spray arcing off their tops when they break, and the birds are flying by, and the whole damn world seems to be at peace with itself, you know you're in the right spot. And as a surfer, you get to sit right smack-dab in the middle of it. Best seat in the house.

The Dangers

But don't let this scene of peace and tranquility lull you into a false sense of security.

There's stuff out there that can cause you serious problems. Sharks seem to be everybody's favorite surfing nightmare, but in the real world they probably wind up somewhere near the very bottom of the list of things that'll get you if you let them. In terms of *real* risk assessment, the chance of getting attacked by a shark is less than that of getting electrocuted by your hair dryer. So don't worry about the sharks. Unless, of course, the water is churning with schools of baitfish and you can see the beasts cutting through them and causing great clouds of 'em to explode out of the water all over the place. Generally speaking, though, you're a helluva lot safer out in the water with the sharks than you are in your car driving down to the beach in the first place.

Sharks, however, aren't the whole story. Currents in the water drag an amazing number of people out to sea, never to be seen again. And for some reason most folks pay this threat very little mind. The subject of currents is sufficiently complex, and sufficiently entangled with other physical properties of large bodies of salt water, that it will be covered in greater detail later in the book.

How about your surfboard? It, too, can be a hazard. A good clonk on the head isn't anybody's idea of fun. Again, this one is going to get covered in greater detail later on.

Hypothermia is another danger to beware of—although chances are pretty good that if the water's cold enough to be a hypothermia risk, and you don't have a good wetsuit on, you're probably not going to be in the water in the first place. Brrrrrrr.

During the summer months along the East Coast, and in Florida in particular, lightning is a real hazard. This is another threat that people don't take seriously enough. When storms start building up over land, and thunder begins growling off in the distance, it's time to get the hell out of the water. If you go waiting around until the lightning starts popping close by, and the thunder starts getting that crisp crackle to it, then you're in the zone. Down on the beach is one of the very best places in the world to get struck by lightning. Lightning kills people on the beach every summer.

Jellyfish can be another problem. They probably won't kill you, but they are fully capable of sending you or your kids to the hospital. Sometimes jellyfish swarm in the water for no understood reason. If they're teeming in the ocean on a particular day, pick another day to surf. In Florida there's the additional threat of Portuguese man-of-wars, but you'll probably never see one in California or Hawaii. People with allergies to the neurotoxin in their tentacles can die from man-of-war stings. If you see any pretty, dark blue to purplish "balloons" on the beach or in the water, stay back. You don't need the trouble. In

Australia they've also got things called cube jellies or sea wasps that are lethal—and you don't have to be allergic to the venom.

Since, clearly, different threats are found in different areas, you should ask the locals about any particular hazards that you might encounter in the water. It pays to do a little homework before you jump in. Go down to the local surfshop or beach park and ask around. Don't be shy about appearing dumb. The only dumb questions are the ones that don't get asked.

Above all, exercise a little common sense. For example, don't pick a beach with waves crashing across shallow reefs and exposed rocks sticking up out of the water.

The Social Life

One of the appeals of surfing is the sense of community you'll find with other surfers. Despite the fact that surfing is done solo and whenever the mood or groundswell strikes, there's a lot of camaraderie among surfers. Once you progress beyond the stage of floundering

Typical surfing scene, Cocoa Beach, Florida.

(photo credit: James MacLaren)

around and getting bashed up by every wave that comes your way, you'll enter the community of other surfers. These are people who'll begin to relate to you in terms of surfing. And believe me, it's a whole other world.

You're going to become a member of the clan. As with any other clan, there are endless subgroups that may or may not get along with each other and may or may not have the least bit of respect for each other. Be that as it may, you'll nonetheless be included within the overarching group. And what a group it is.

Surfing is a strong attraction for free spirits and rugged individualists. Not everybody out in the water glurping around on a surfboard is some kind of Jack London monolith, but there's definitely a greater percentage of such folks in the population of surfers than there is in the general population.

And most of these people are pretty neat to be around. Real characters. Often I find myself hanging around on the beach after a surf session for a greater length of time than I spent in the water actually surfing. Just hanging out.

Equipment

Despite the common image of the surfer as standing upright on a surfboard while she rides the waves, there are other approaches to the sport. Of the three main branches of surfing, two of them leave the rider in a prone position.

Which branch of surfing you indulge in is wholly dependent on the equipment you choose to ride.

This section will discuss not only the gear you ride but also the gear you may need for other aspects of surfing.

We'll start with boards you stand on and work down from there.

Bodyboard (left), longboard (center), shortboard (right).

(photo credit: James MacLaren)

Surfboards

Basically, surfboards come in three flavors: long, short, and soft. Each has its advantages and its drawbacks.

Longboards

For the novice surfer, the one who wants to stand up and surf the way most people think is the only way to do it, longboards are the way to go. For the purposes of getting introduced to the sport, longboards are all gain and almost no loss.

In general, a long surfboard is anything over 8 feet in length. Practically speaking, however, don't bother with anything less than 9 feet long. Get a big board. One that really floats you well. Of course, if you weigh 60 pounds sopping wet, a shorter board is okay. You'll float just fine.

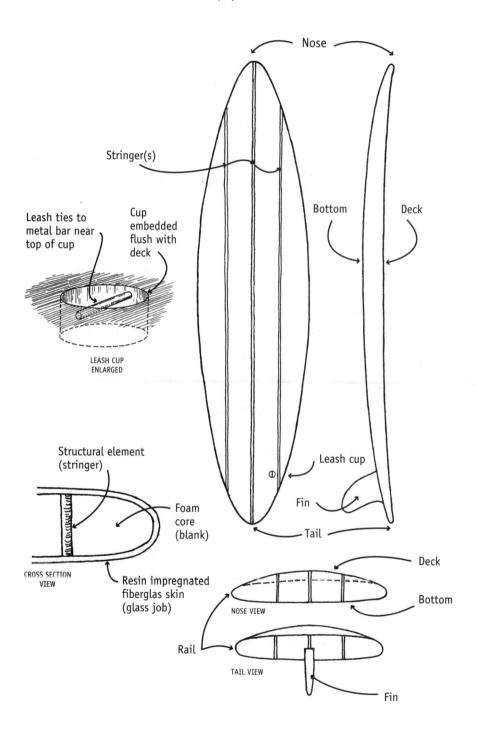

Nose

Stringer(s)

Bottom

Deck

Leash ties to metal bar near top of cup

Cup embedded flush with deck

LEASH CUP
ENLARGED

Structural element (stringer)

Foam core (blank)

CROSS SECTION
VIEW

Resin impregnated fiberglas skin (glass job)

Leash cup

Fin

Tail

Deck

Bottom

NOSE VIEW

Rail

TAIL VIEW

Fin

Longboards are superior for a whole slew of reasons. They handle much more steadily on a wave. Their flotation allows you to learn to paddle with greater ease. They catch waves more quickly and easily. They allow smaller (and safer) waves to be ridden. They're more forgiving of control errors when you're riding a wave. All of these reasons (and more) just shout to the neophyte surfer: Get a longboard.

About the only drawbacks to longboards are tied directly to their largeness. They're unwieldy to drag to the beach and back. You'll have to get a set of surf racks for your car (we'll discuss these a little later) to transport your longboard if you're not staying in a place right on the beach or don't have a van or something similar in which to tote it around. Longboards also give a bigger and better clonk when you get hit by them. A longboard can really knock you silly if you let it.

Shortboards

Shortboards are the Ferraris of the surfing world. And as you might guess, putting somebody who's never driven a car behind the wheel of such a high-powered, high-strung device isn't such a good idea.

Shortboards are for people who know how to surf already. Yes, it is possible to learn to surf on a shortboard, but why make an already difficult assignment even more so?

The desire to hop on a shortboard from the very get-go seems to afflict people in their middle teens the most. After all, one look at a crowd of surfers in the water will reveal that the coolest of the cool are almost all riding shortboards. The thought of getting out in front of all those cool people on a big clunky board that looks like it came right out of one of those stupid beach blanket bobo movies is enough to give your average 13-year-old a case of the hives.

However, all things considered, the case of hives is preferable to the frustrations and hazards associated with learning to surf on a short surfboard.

The one exception to this rule kicks in when the person learning to surf is about six or seven years old. Little guys like this float on a shortboard the way you or I would float on something that looks like it was bought surplus from the U.S. Navy.

The actual drawbacks to learning on a shortboard are that they're difficult to paddle and extremely squirrelly to handle. When you get right down to it, you don't really even paddle a shortboard. You're more *swimming* it than anything else, and that's no picnic. It's real work just to get from here to there. And when it comes to actually catching a wave, you're almost in a position where you have to let the wave catch you. Attempting to come to your feet on any surfboard just as a breaking wave pummels you is no easy trick. And a shortboard is so susceptible to your movements it will go everywhere but where you want it to as you flail around trying to merely stay on top of the thing.

Skip the shortboard. At least until you have a better grasp on surfing.

Softboards

Softboards are an excellent alternative for learning to surf. The overriding advantage of a soft surfboard is *safety*. Softies are constructed differently than your average surfboard. Normal boards are hard and rigid. This allows them to cut through the water with maximum efficiency. Softboards are made from a spongelike material. Which type of board would you rather get knocked upside the head with? The trade-off comes in the efficiency with which a softboard cuts through the water.

Most softboards are on the longish side, about 7 to 8 feet long. The people who make them already know that serious surfers are going to be slashing around in the water on something else. Softboard manufacturers generally build a product aimed at the newbies in the surfing world. Like maybe your Aunt Nellie from Topeka. *Anybody* can learn to surf on a softboard.

The problem with them is that you'll outgrow them as soon as you master the very basics of the sport. Nobody, but nobody, stays with a softie once she's figured out the minimal moves of surfing. Yes indeed, softboards handle *that much worse* than regular surfboards. And if you stay on your softboard, don't plan on progressing very far in your surfing abilities. Softboards set fixed limits beyond which you cannot go.

The place for softboards in your surfing universe should be in the rental shop. On your very first day in the water, it's fine to be on a softboard, even desirable. But don't buy one. If it turns out that the surfing bug bites you, you'll want to be on a regular surfboard as soon as possible. If, for whatever reason, surfing isn't for you, you'll be glad you merely rented a softboard instead of having shelled out the bucks to purchase one.

surf Racks

Now that you know what kind of board you want to use, how are you going to get it down to the beach?

If you've got a shortboard, you can very likely just put it inside your car and off you go. But, as stated above, I recommend you stay off the shortboard till you've figured out the surfing basics. And in order to lug around a longboard or a softie, you'll need a set of surf racks.

Surf racks are specialty items made for the specific purpose of securing your surfboard(s) to the roof of your car. There are two types: hard and soft. Which type you decide on is up to you.

Hard racks have the advantage of being more or less permanently attached to the roof of your car. Whenever you take a notion to throw your board on the roof and blast off to the beach, the racks are already in place, waiting for you to tie your board to them. Hard racks are more durable, too. Your board is less likely to take flight suddenly and commit suicide into a telephone pole alongside the road. However, some people don't like the look of a set of surf racks messing up the racy silhouette of the car they just spent all that money on. Also, racks that stay on the roof of your car while you're out in the water surfing are vulnerable to anybody who wants to unscrew and steal them.

Soft racks.

(photo credit: James MacLaren)

Soft racks have the advantage of being removable. Since they consist of nothing more than some nylon strapping, rubber pads, and a couple of clips, they can be stuffed into your trunk or under the front seat of your car. Poof, and they're gone. No theft problems with soft racks, unless you forget and leave them on the car when you go out surfing. If you're traveling somewhere and expect to be putting surfboards on top of a rental car, soft racks are indispensable. Just stuff 'em into one of your suitcases and off you go. But soft racks are also more of a hassle to deal with—you've got to attach them to your car every time you use them. A set of snarled-up soft racks can be a real pain to untangle and get properly secured.

Another drawback of soft racks is that they're more prone to come loose and send your expensive surfboard on a flight of doom as you're whamming down the road. Tie 'em on there good or else you and the driver next to you whose open window receives your errant surfboard will be sorry.

Cords

An indispensable item for people learning to surf is a cord. Cords are shock-absorbing lines that attach around your ankle with a Velcro cuff on one end, and tie to the rear of your surfboard on the other. With a cord, you'll never become separated from your surfboard. You'll never have to swim like a seal to retrieve it from waves and currents that are carrying it off. Cords also prevent your lost surfboard from being hurled by a wave and nailing some poor slob in the head as she's paddling out into the waves. Most surfers these days use a cord. You should too.

Cords can also cause trouble, however, so you've got to be careful when you're using one. After you fall off your surfboard (something you'll be doing a lot of till you get the hang of surf-

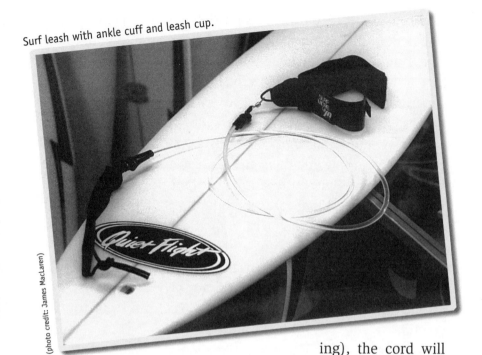

Surf leash with ankle cuff and leash cup.

(photo credit: James MacLaren)

ing), the cord will stretch out and then yank the board right back at you. This is nice when it comes to not having to swim for the board, but it's not so nice when it comes to getting the stuffing knocked out of you by the rebounding surfboard. And more often than not when you come up from underwater after falling off your surfboard, the only part of you above water for the board to knock silly is, you guessed it, your head.

Not only that, but since the cord is attached to the rear of the surfboard (for good reasons, which you'll learn in a moment), the part of the board that'll be aiming for your temple is the part of the board with the fins on it.

All of this is to say *be careful* when coming up from underwater after taking a spill. The main technique for avoiding trouble with the surfboard when you're surfacing after a wipeout is simply a matter of being aware of any pressure exerted by the cord on your ankle. If the cord is pulling away for all it's worth then you can rest assured that the other end of it, the one that's attached to the surfboard, is doing the exact same thing there. Wait around underwater for a bit and let some slack develop in the cord, if you can. If there's steady tension on the cord and you've run out of air and need to surface, just remember that the cord is pulling the board toward your ankle. The main thing is to keep your head from getting between your surfboard and your ankle. Putting an arm over your head as you break the surface will probably be sufficient to ward off the board.

Something else that cords do is become tangled around your feet as you attempt to stand atop the board. This tangle factor is why the cord is attached to the *rear* of the board. While you're traveling through the water the cord tends to get dragged rearward behind the board, where it's out of your way. If it was attached to the nose of the board it would constantly be tripping you up.

Which leg you will tie the cord to depends on which of your legs is farthest to the rear as you stand on top of the surfboard. Your stance on a surfboard when riding waves is with your feet planted *crosswise* to your direction of travel. Both feet are placed over the centerline of the board, one in front, one in back. Which foot winds up in front is purely a personal matter. Most (not all) right-handed people surf with their left foot forward; the reverse is true for most (not all) left-handed people. Whichever way is more comfortable and feels more natural is the way you want to do it. Determine which foot is your rear foot and attach the cord to that leg.

Don't allow any of the information you've just learned to give you second thoughts about using a cord. For the beginning surfer, it's *essential.* Keep in mind that if you're being pulled along to some awful place by waves or currents, it's your cord that's going to be keeping you in contact with your handy dandy personal flotation device—your surfboard. Cords are the single most important piece of safety equipment for neophyte surfers. Get a cord and learn to use it.

Wax/Traction Pads

Another absolutely essential piece of your surfing equipment is something to provide you with the traction you'll need to keep your feet from slipping off the wet surface of your surfboard. Most surfboards (softies excepted) come fresh from the factory with a highly polished

(photo credit: James MacLaren)

Surfwax.

finish. They're real shiny and neat looking. The slick finish helps them cut through the water with minimal drag, makes them go faster. But it also makes a board impossible to stand on when wet. Don't even try. Wax gives you traction. So do traction pads, but they're usually placed only on part of the board, and you've still got to wax the rest of the board anyway.

Surfwax is a whole little world unto itself. You've got to get your hands on some surfwax in order to learn what to do with it. If you picked up your surfboard at a surfshop, ask the person at the counter about wax. Be sure not to get anything with the word *tacky* on it. Tacky wax is dynamite traction but it'll also give you the worst rash of your life when you lie on it to paddle. If you're wearing a full wetsuit, tacky wax is fine. Otherwise, forget it. Really, though, you don't need tacky wax until your surfing improves dramatically. Standard surfwax is just fine. Even a bar of paraffin will do in a pinch. Don't use candle wax, though; it's too greasy.

If you're not at the surfshop, don't worry. Down by the beach in any of the towns where surfing is done, surfwax is almost always available in any of the little minimarkets that dot the highway. Just go in and ask for it. A bar should cost you around a dollar.

Now that you've got your hands on the bar of wax, let's go put it on your surfboard. If the board you're using already has some wax on it, you still need to wax it. Wax the board *every* time you go surfing. There's no substitute for good traction, and the more the better.

First, be careful not to lay the board out in the hot sun where it'll get so warm that the wax turns to goo as you're trying to apply it. Now take the bar of wax and just rub it around on the top surface of the surfboard, *not* the bottom.

Cover the top surface of the board with wax. Don't worry about the very front end of the board. You're never going to be standing up there, and even if you do wind up there by mistake, all the traction in the world isn't going to save you from the thrashing you'll take in the next half a second.

Don't overwax the board. At some point you'll notice that your bar of wax is scraping off as much wax as it's putting on. When that happens move to another place on the board. After you've been out in the water and wallowing around on the board for a while, check the wax job. Sometimes you'll find you've worked the wax off the board in spots. If the wax is gone, or gets thin, put more on. Maximum traction is what you want.

Occasionally the wax on the board will become slick and won't give you the traction you need. Surfshops sell wax combs that you can use to rough up the slicked-over surface of an otherwise acceptable wax job. In a pinch you can take a bit of sand and rub it over the wax while the board is in the water; it'll scuff up the slicked-over wax enough to restore good traction. However, this is a tricky procedure and takes some folks a while to get the hang of.

There's more to wax than just knowing how to apply it to your surfboard correctly. The stuff is horribly messy and if it melts into the carpet on the floorboards of your expensive new car, you can forget about getting it all out. It's there to stay. So don't leave a bar of wax exposed to direct sunlight inside your locked car on a hot day. It'll turn into a nasty liquid and flow downhill onto whatever's most expensive and intolerant of contaminants. Put your wax in the pocket of your surf trunks when you're surfing. Be sure to take it out of the surf trunks when you get home, though. A bar of surfwax left in clothing that goes through the laundry is an utter disaster. It'll ruin whatever's in the laundry with it, and possibly the washer or dryer, too.

Needless to say, everything terrible that applies to your bar of surfwax also applies to your waxed surfboard. Not that you'll put your board through the washer and dryer, but do avoid leaving it around in direct sunlight on hot days; it'll ooze wax all over the place when it gets hot. Not only will this destroy the upholstery in your car, but you'll also have to reapply a whole coat of wax to your board. But, don't worry, you'll get the hang of handling wax after using it a few times.

Traction pads are sheets of textured material that you attach to the pristine *unwaxed* surface of your board using a waterproof adhesive. They're available in surfshops. You can get them in thin or thick models and in different sizes, shapes, and patterns. Mostly they're used by people who already surf reasonably well, to provide maximum traction for that spot on the tail of their surfboards where their power foot is always planted. Some people plaster their entire boards with them. Others don't like traction pads anywhere on their boards. I don't like the feel of them under me as I paddle the board. Nor do I like tripping over 'em as I'm walking around on my board. You won't have to worry about walking around all over your board for a long time, but whether or not you want to mess around with traction pads is a decision you'll have to make for yourself.

(photo credit: James MacLaren)

Shortboards with traction pads.

Bodyboards Bodyboards are an alternative, something you're *supposed* to lie down on. With none of the difficulties associated with having to stand up on a surfboard, bodyboards allow you to try your luck with surfing on a much easier level.

Bodyboards are soft and spongelike, so you can't get hurt by one if it hits you. The waves you'll likely be riding one on are going to be breaking nice and close to the beach, so it won't be a big deal if you lose the bodyboard in a wipeout. Just run to the beach and grab it, and it's back out for more fun and games you go.

With a bodyboard you just push out into the waves while lying on it, turn around, and take the next wave in.

But there are a few drawbacks to be aware of.

Bodyboards are *extremely* difficult to paddle, even with a set of swimfins on your feet. The flotation afforded by a bodyboard is almost nonexistent. They sink down into the water when you paddle and the instant you stop paddling or kicking with the fins, you stop dead in the water. If you're just starting out with surfing, the poor paddling characteristics of bodyboards can be very frustrating. You don't go anywhere. You just flail around and wear yourself out without really making much forward progress. It's best to *walk* a bodyboard most of the way out to where the waves are breaking, and then either jump into them to catch them, or take a very few paddling strokes while kicking with your swimfins to get in the wave.

Bodyboards, however, are a blast in conditions where the surf comes out of deep water, encounters a shallow sandbar just off the beach, and explodes like a bomb. The surfing term for these sorts of waves is *shorebreak.* Shorebreak is useless for beginners on regular surfboards, but it's loads of fun on a body-board.

If you're stuck in a locale where the waves are pounding shorebreak, a bodyboard just might be your best route for learning to surf—at least as long as the waves are breaking over a sandy bottom. Don't even think about trying this sort of thing with a powerful shorebreak that's working over a shallow, *rock* bottom. That's a sure way to end up in the hospital.

Folks who surf really well can do some amazing things with a bodyboard. But for now forget all about trying fancy maneuvers. It takes years to get good at bodyboarding. Just be happy with cruising along into the shorebreak and getting whomped. That's plenty fun for starters.

Bodyboards, while less expensive than surfboards, aren't cheap. If you're thinking about purchasing a bodyboard, you've got a few things to consider before doing so. You'll probably want to rent one from a surfshop or somewhere else at the beach to see if it's something you'll want to keep using. Pick a day with what you think are at least half-decent waves (shorebreak, not too small, but not big enough to drown you either) when making this decision. Bodyboards don't go anywhere on 6-inch waves.

The first question you should ask yourself when considering a purchase is, "How bad do I want to learn to surf?" If you're not sure about the whole thing, don't go blowing a C-note on a top-of-the-line bodyboard. Pick up one of the inexpensive models at the surfshop or buy one used. You might even find one priced right at a garage sale.

Another purchase to consider is swimfins. If you're not yet sure you want to learn to bodyboard, forget the fins. When you do decide it's lots of fun and you want more, then the fins will be a necessity. Swimfins will be covered in more detail later on.

Without the fins you're basically limited to staying in water that's shallow enough to walk out to where you'll be surfing. This places you in much smaller surf, but since you're just learning and don't want to get the living wazoodium knocked out of you, that's probably for the best. Should the small waves you're riding not provide enough thrill, get the fins. But be careful. It's dangerous out there in the deep water. And by the way, *dive fins are strictly prohibited.* (See below for further description.) They don't work well and you'll very likely lose them the first time you take a good wipeout.

Swimfin (top) and dive fin (bottom).

(photo credit: James MacLaren)

Fins Only (Bodysurfing)

Time for some minimalist art. It's perfectly possible to surf without benefit of any sort of board whatsoever. Bodysurfing. Your own personal and private body is equipment enough to allow a wave to carry you along with it to the beach.

Although it *is* possible to bodysurf without benefit of fins, it's a whole lot more fun if you're wearing a nice pair of swimfins. Again, not dive fins. Swimfins. They're different.

Dive fins are fairly thin and have a large surface area. This makes them perfect for languidly kicking along, 30 feet down, among the coral heads and moray eels. Swimfins for bodysurfing and bodyboarding look strange to anyone who thinks dive fins are what fins ought to look like. A good pair of fins for bodysurfing has less surface area than dive fins do. They're also thick along the sides and made of flexible rubber instead of the stiffer plastic that dive fins are usually made of. The short, stubby design maximizes propulsion when you're sprint kicking to get into a wave. The ends of the swimfins may be cut on a diagonal. This places the maximum amount of fin (giving you maximum control) in the wave as you ride it.

Swimfins aren't as readily available as most other surfing equipment. Many surfshops don't stock them. If the shop you go to doesn't have a pair of swimfins—Churchill's are widely considered to be the best—ask the folks there to steer you in the direction of someplace that does. You might have to order them through the mail. For this, get your hands on a surf magazine (there are several different ones out there) and root around through the ads till you find swimfins.

Another item to consider is a pair of little cords with cuffs that go around your ankles on one end, and attach to the swimfins on the other. Should a fin get yanked off in a wipeout, you won't lose it. I never bodysurf without mine.

If getting a whole new set of fins just to bodysurf seems like too much hassle, you *can* use those dive fins that are stuffed somewhere in the back of the hall closet. But they won't work nearly as well. And there's a much greater chance that they'll be yanked off your feet by a wave. If you *must* use dive fins, be sure to get a set with a strap that goes around the back of your ankle, as opposed to the kind with a closed heel. Those with a closed heel always get jerked off and lost.

Riding a wave using fins only will be covered later on.

Surf Trunks/Bathing suits

What were you planning on wearing while you learned to surf? Had it even occurred to you that perhaps something specialized would be required?

While it's true that you can try your luck on a surfboard in those old cutoff jeans or a two-piece, you're better off wearing something a bit more appropriate to the task at hand.

There's not really much to it; you just need to be aware that as part of your surfing education you're going to be heading through some serious rinse cycles along the way. Tailor your garb to suit.

For women, it boils down to "Don't wear a two-piece bathing suit." Unless it's one of those two-piece jobs that's built to *really* stay on. However, you're better off wearing a one-piece bathing suit when learning to surf.

Baggies.

Men need to wear appropriate clothing when surfing, too. Surf trunks (they're called baggies by surfers) can be picked up at just about any surfshop in sizes up to about 40. Larger than that, they're harder to come by. Through mail order via the ads in surf magazines, though, they can be had in all sizes. Don't begrudge the expenditure of money on a pair of baggies. They can double as a pair of walking shorts. Better, actually, since they're more durable. Surf trunks are built with good strong closures (laces or snaps in most cases) and a loose fit otherwise. With all the twisting and turning you're going to be doing while learning to surf, anything that restricts where it shouldn't is going to be placed under a terrific strain. This is why cutoff jeans aren't a good idea. Standard bathing suit trunks usually don't fit closely enough and are likely to come off during a wipeout.

Baggies are the way to go. Be sure to get a pair that has a good pocket to keep your surfwax in. For this reason, some women wear them, too.

Wetsuits

If the water's cold, you'll need a wetsuit. Cold water will conduct heat away from your body at an alarming rate. The only thing in common between 65-degree air and 65-degree water is the number. Sixty-five-degree water is *much* colder than 65-degree air. Depending on your metabolism and your general state of health, water in the low 60s and below is a potential killer. You don't want to die from hypothermia. Wear a wetsuit.

Wetsuits come in all shapes and sizes, for women, men, and children. Once again, if you're not sure how serious you are about surfing, pick up a used wetsuit. Ask around among the folks at the surfshop. They'd rather sell you a new one off the rack, but if they're nice people they might clue you in to somebody who's got a used one to cut loose at a nice cheap price.

If you're in an area with cold water and you think you can try surfing without the wetsuit, to see if you really want to learn it, *stop this very minute.* Don't even think about it! Sitting atop your surfboard, soaking wet, experiencing a windchill factor you never imagined, there's no way you're ever going to try surfing again.

Wetsuits are tailored for the various conditions found around the globe at different surf-spots—everything from a cloudy day in Hawaii to February in Maine. Be sure to get the right wetsuit for your area and conditions.

Fullsuit, springsuit, and vest.

(photo credit: James MacLaren)

For the cloudy day in Hawaii, or even an early cold spell in Florida (*before* the water temperature has dropped below 80 degrees), a wetsuit vest is all you'll need. It covers your torso so the wind doesn't give your wet body a chill. Vests come sleeveless or with short sleeves, depending on your preference.

For warm-water conditions when the air is a bit on the chilly side, there's the springsuit. Springsuits cover your torso and have short legs that allow them to cover the lower portion of your torso better. They may or may not have long sleeves to help ward off the chill of that cold air that's blowing across your exposed body.

For the cold-water conditions with warm air that are so common in California, there's the long john. A long john is essentially a vest that keeps going, all the way down to your ankles. Sitting on top of your board in the warm air, you don't need to worry about your torso getting chilled, and the long legs take care of the evil effects of the cold water.

Cold water with cold air (anywhere in the mainland United States in winter, except south of Palm Beach in Florida) requires full coverage: a fullsuit. From the neck down, out to your wrists and down to your ankles, you're covered. *Real* cold water? Add booties. Arctic air? Get gloves and a hood.

For the horrific conditions of the northeastern U.S. in the dead of winter, you'll probably need a dry suit. Dry suits allow you to enter the water fully dressed. They cover everything and have watertight seals that won't let that freezing-cold water come into direct contact with your pitiful body. Dry suits don't really belong in this book because *nobody* is going to attempt to learn to surf in a place that has snow on the beach. Go skiing. Save the surf session till next summer.

If you still have questions about what to wear, you can ask around at the surfshop for helpful advice. Or you can just have a look at what most of the people already out in the water have on and wear the same thing. Suit yourself.

Sunscreen/shirts/Hats/sunglasses

You'll need all the junk you usually bring along with you to the beach, for all the same reasons.

Sunscreen is essential. If you go down to the beach on a sunny day and surf (or just flounder around) for a couple of hours, you're going to get the sunburn of your life if you didn't apply sunscreen before hitting the beach.

The ultraviolet rays coming from the sun are reflected back at you by the sand and water, greatly magnified. This includes days with milky, hazy skies that you can't even properly see the sun through. The UV rays cut through the clouds and can burn you as much as they can—sometimes worse—on a clear sunny day, because you don't feel the heat, and you tend to think that nothing's happening. You'll have a big surprise when you get home.

Get sunscreen with a high sunblock factor and be sure it's *waterproof*. Another thing to be careful about with your sunscreen is that it's not oily. When surfing, any sunscreen that leaves a film of slick oil on your skin will get all over the deck of your surfboard and completely negate the salutary effects of that A1 wax job you spent so much time getting just right.

What you want is something that gets absorbed into your skin and disappears without a trace. It's out there, you just need to look for it.

Cover yourself literally from head to toe with the sunscreen. This includes out-of-the-way areas like the tops of your ears.

A surprising amount of your time spent surfing will be spent not surfing. You'll wear yourself out in short order flailing away on the old surfboard. It's a real workout. And once you're tired, you'll need to recharge your batteries hanging around on the beach. And when you're sitting it out on the beach, you'll be glad to have your shirt, sunscreen, sunglasses, and hat.

Broad-brim hats, and Panama hats with extra-wide brims, are recommended. Just about anything will do so long as it provides the greatest amount of shade. Don't make a big investment in your hat. It should be something you won't mind globbing up with surfwax or beach tar by mistake.

Shirts are useful for keeping the sun from burning a hole in you. Some people, after they've dried off and all that's left on their skin is that crust of salt, can't tolerate the close, unpleasant sensation of wearing a shirt. Especially on a hot day. If you're one of these types (as I am), then be sure to really lay on the waterproof sunscreen with a heavy hand. Otherwise, wear the shirt.

But beware. A shirt all by itself won't do the trick. Not only does it not cover extremely important areas like the nape of your neck and the tops of your ears, but even the part of you it does cover remains vulnerable to ultraviolet rays. The thin cotton of most T-shirts will provide protection that's the equivalent of sunblock factor 8. So, again, wear the sunscreen.

Make sure your sunglasses block ultraviolet rays. Without this UV protection sunglasses are worse than useless. A pair of shades that doesn't block UV will trick your pupils into opening wider than they would ordinarily, exposing them to UV rays that can damage your retinas. Protection is worth the effort and cost.

Where to Surf

Now that you know what you need to wear and the gear you'll be using, let's go down to the water and get going.

Beaches

Going down to the water involves the matter of choosing exactly where you want to go. It's not enough that you head in the general direction of the ocean. You've got to find the right stretch of beach on which to learn to surf.

Beaches come in a bewildering array: everything from 1,000-foot cliffs with waves the size of apartment buildings bashing against their bases all the way down to endless stretches of sand that slope ever-so-gently out into waveless waters. As well as more combinations of the above, intermediate forms, and otherwise unclassifiable mutants than you can shake a surfboard at.

Here's what you're looking for: *A nice sandy beach that slopes gently and evenly out into the water where waist-high waves are breaking softly and rolling steadily toward shore.*

Try to avoid beaches where there are lots of rocks. Rocks with waves breaking on them can cause damage to you and your surfboard. If you *must* surf among rocks, pick a place where the breaking waves (rolling walls of whitewater) completely peter out before they encounter any exposed rocks. And don't go where the rocks are sharp and jagged. Smooth-rock bottoms (especially if the rocks are covered in soft seaweed) aren't so very bad—but again, not where the waves are hitting the exposed rocks with any vigor.

Not all sand beaches are okay, either. Avoid places with a deep trough running along near the beach where the whitewater fades out and the waves come right up to the beach, gather themselves up, and then plunge over with a noticeable *whump* in just a few inches of water. Places like that will knock you silly and the only thing you'll ever learn about surfing is that it's dangerous and no fun at all.

Pick your beach with care and forethought. If there's a place around where little kids and old men are surfing, that's probably where you want to be, too.

For instance, if you're on Easter Island, Anakena Beach is perfect. Anywhere else, and you'll die. If you're in Florida, just about anywhere at all is okeydokey unless the surf is dead flat (which happens an appalling number of days out of the year). In California, you're going to have to scope out the local lay of the land. California has just about everything and you'll need to be careful to pick somewhere safe.

Safe is the word to keep in mind.

In Hawaii, go to Waikiki and pay one of the beachboys to give you proper lessons. They know more about surfing than anyone else and will give you the best possible education. The guys on the beach at Waikiki are a national treasure of surfing lore and you should feel privileged just to be allowed to go out in the same ocean as them. Be sure to give a generous tip when you're done.

Wipeout!

Anywhere else in Hawaii for your first attempt at surfing and *forget it!* Unless you grew up there. Except maybe Kailua Beach or someplace similar, with nice soft sand and small gentle waves.

Surf camps and schools are becoming more popular. If there's one in your area, check it out. You may or may not be willing to shell out the requisite bucks to enroll. But you should have a look, at least.

Never try to tackle more than you can handle your first few times out in the ocean.

Here's a true story: One day, years ago, a guy came floundering past me on a big, clunky rental surfboard. He could hardly stay on top of the thing as he paddled it. If it wasn't his very first day on a surfboard, it wasn't too far from it. This would have been fine except for one small detail. I was sitting in the lineup, waiting for the next set of waves, at a spot on the North Shore called Waimea Bay. It was a medium-small day for the bay. We were calling the waves 12 feet. You'd call them 20. My friend, the novice, actually managed to get in among the crowd of surfers and start paddling for a wave. Impossibly, the wave caught him! He started down the face of it and, upon realizing what he'd gotten mixed up with, rolled off the side of his rental surfboard. The board continued on its merry way all the way to the bottom of the wave where it *just* missed two other surfers who were charging along from farther back on the wave. Nobody got hurt, but they easily could have.

If there's anything more complex **Waves** than all the different types of beaches there are, it's the waves that are breaking at those beaches.

If you've never really *looked* at waves, then you're at a disadvantage. The good news is that everything's right there in the open for you to get a good look at, though the differences are often subtle and easily overlooked by the untrained eye.

Basically, waves come in from deep water as rollers then encounter the shallow water near shore and break, forming a wall of whitewater that pushes into the beach and dissipates.

There are many ways this process can occur.

Sometimes waves don't break at all. When they encounter cliff faces that plunge on down into deep water, swells just bounce off the faces without ever breaking.

Sometimes waves break when they're not supposed to. A strong wind blowing against the back of a wave will cause it to occasionally topple over and form whitewater, even in the middle of the ocean where the water is a mile deep.

Sometimes waves encounter shallow water far from shore and break, only to back off after they cross over the shallow zone and reenter deep water. Places like this will have a line of whitewater far from shore, and an area of green water closer in where the waves aren't breaking anymore. Sometimes there's more than one reef or sandbar, and the process will be repeated several times over. Each time a wave breaks, it expends some of its energy. When a wave re-forms, it does so at a smaller size.

Waves can break so hard that they give the impression of a bomb going off, or they can crumble gently and easily with little fanfare, hissing to their deaths as thin sheets of water on the sand.

And of course any and all of the above can occur in combination. The same beach can offer wildly different wave types depending upon wind, tide, and swell conditions.

A fundamental item that must be understood in order to understand waves is *wind*. Waves are children of the wind. The wind gives birth to waves and shapes them for their entire lives. When the wind blows in the same direction the waves are traveling in, it creates a choppy, disorganized condition. Winds coming onto the shore from out over the ocean are called *onshore winds.* Conditions of onshore wind can create waves, but those waves will not be as good for riding as the alternative kind.

Winds blowing off the shore, from land toward sea and against the direction that the waves are moving in, are called *offshore winds.* These are by far the better of the two alternatives. Offshore winds brush the surface of the ocean smooth and cause the waves to come in as graceful, even rollers. No chop. No disorganization.

It's a good idea to memorize *onshore* and *offshore* winds. They're of critical importance to the rest of the picture.

Onshore: Wind blowing from the sea into your face as you stand on the shore and watch the waves coming in toward you. A wind that blows in the same direction the waves are traveling in.

Offshore: Wind blowing out to sea from the land, against your back as you stand watching the waves come in. A wind blowing in the opposite direction from that the waves are traveling in.

Things to Look For

The waves you want to go out on for your first lessons in surfing on your longboard are the waves that crumble gently—as opposed to the ones that go off like a bomb.

Look for a setup where small waves are washing gently toward a beach that has a nice, shallow slope that dips off, ever so gently and evenly, below the level of the water.

A setup like this means a much kinder, gentler energy release as the waves break. Waves that have a tendency to plunge over with lots of vigor, creating a *tube* as they break, are not what you want. Those are more than a beginner can handle.

An even slope of the sandy bottom as it deepens going out to sea is important, too. Many beaches have a pronounced trough running parallel to shore where the water gets quite deep. Not only can this deep trough serve as a hole in which to fall and drown, it also messes up the waves for beginners. Waves that encounter a deep trough close to shore quit breaking. You can't ride waves that just sink down into the sea.

Worse, spots like this are usually just shoreward of where the surf is breaking along nicely, in shallower water. The problem arises when it's too deep for you to walk the board out to where the breakers are. Instead, you must paddle. Paddling is difficult, a real workout. When you're still learning, it's unlikely that you'll be able to paddle across that deep trough and out to where the waves are breaking. What happens is that even as the broken whitewaters are about to peter out, they still have more than enough power to impede your progress seaward. And so you'll be stuck, just at the outer edge of the trough, fighting against whitewater that keeps slapping you back toward shore. But as soon as you give up, turn the board back around to where it's pointing shoreward, and attempt to catch a wave, you'll get a frustrating surprise. By virtue of your unfortunate location at the outer edge of the trough, you'll be sitting *exactly* in the wrong spot. Every wave you attempt to catch (even when they're actually hitting you from behind as breaking walls of whitewater) will instantly glurp down into the deep water of the trough and become completely unsurfable!

The best-case scenario in a situation like this is annoyance. The worst-case is far more serious. After becoming enraged with the ocean out on the outer edge of the trough, you may decide to paddle in to where the waves are breaking right on the shore. And by now, you'll be tired, irritable, and not really paying attention to *how* those waves are breaking on the shore. Places where there's a pronounced trough usually have a bitter end where the waves come out of their sulk in the trough, rise up, and dash themselves to oblivion in one last spasm of fury right on the beach in mere *inches* of water. This last gasp is, again, called *the shorebreak*. Never attempt to learn to surf in the shorebreak; it's too dangerous. It'll hurl you and your surfboard violently into the surprisingly hard-packed sand that lurks mere inches below the surface of the water that the wave is pile-driving you down into. Situations like this can result in your getting smashed by the impact of your surfboard, or worse—the same damage can be inflicted on unheeding children and adults splishing around in the ankle-deep water just ahead of where your final ride of the day comes to its inglorious end.

Instead, find yourself a sand-bottom place where you can walk out to knee to waist depth. A place without any intervening deep-water trough. A place where the waves are just a foot or two high and crumbling softly toward the shore.

Someplace safe.

Things to Watch Out For

It's almost time to take the plunge. But before you do, you should be aware of the things to watch out for. Things that could ruin your whole day if you let them.

The ocean is a wilderness. Bigger and wilder than the Amazon basin. Once you pass from the human realm on the beach into the untamed world where the waves are, you're essentially on your own. The ocean doesn't care who you are, how much money you have, or where you came from. Don't lose sight of this vital truth.

If you're a strong swimmer you have an advantage over everybody else. But if you swim poorly, or even not at all, you can still enjoy the pleasures of the surf. The difference lies in knowing the greatest degree of oceanic agitation that you can reasonably expect to survive. Strong swimmers can plunge into churning waves that others may enter only at a very real risk to their well-being.

Fortunately, the best waves for learning to surf are also the safest waves for everybody, the little piddly waves glurping along in knee- to waist-deep water.

These are the waves that everybody should start out in, everybody from Aunt Nellie to Cousin Macho. In a way, Aunt Nellie has the advantage here. She already knows that the ocean can do her harm if she lets it. She can also quite likely take one look at the waves on a given day and instantly determine whether or not she has any business out there among them. Cousin Macho, however, is a different matter. Owing to the fact that he's on the first-string football team, or perhaps has survived basic training in the marines, he thinks he's rough and tough enough to handle whatever the ocean throws his way. He's wrong.

For every Aunt Nellie who gets swept out to sea and lost, there are ten Cousin Machos. Take heed.

Currents will take you wherever they want to. To deal with currents you need to know what to do (and *not* do) when you're in one. As long as you keep your wits about you, there will be no problem.

There are two types of currents. Longshore currents and rip currents. Of the two, longshore currents are much more benign.

To the eyes of most people, waves come directly out of the open sea and travel straight toward the shore that they'll break upon. Surfers' eyes see things a little differently. Often waves can be seen to be heading toward the shore at a slight angle. Some people have no trouble discerning the angle at which waves travel shoreward. Others never figure it out. It doesn't really matter whether or not you're able to see the difference, though; what is important to understand is the *consequence* of waves coming in at an angle.

The Longshore Current

When waves come straight in, the water washes in and out with each passing wave but otherwise remains pretty much in place. Waves coming in at an angle, however, create a longshore current. Not only does the water wash in and out with each wave, it also moves steadily down the beach in one direction or the other. If you toss a rubber ball straight out into the surf and it comes back in somewhere noticeably to the right or left of where you were standing when you threw it out, then you're seeing the effects of longshore current. The current travels along the length of the shore, hence the name.

Longshore currents can be anywhere from barely noticeable to speeding rivers of water. People who go fishing in the surf quickly learn to recognize longshore currents. The current drags their rigs way down the beach and makes for lousy fishing.

For our purposes the longshore current isn't nearly as bothersome. In general, a longshore current won't cause you any more trouble than it takes to lug your surfboard back to where you first entered the water. You've merely drifted down the beach from where you started. No big deal. If the water is really whooshing down the beach at a good clip, however, pick another day to learn to surf. Walking a quarter mile back to where your car is parked while lugging a surfboard after only 15 minutes in the water isn't much fun. Not only that, but when

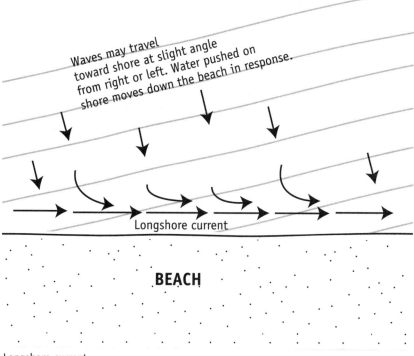

Waves may travel toward shore at slight angle from right or left. Water pushed on shore moves down the beach in response.

Longshore current

BEACH

Longshore current.

the current is really cutting along, it means there's a pretty good swell pushing it. Probably too much surf for a beginner. In conditions like this it's wise to heed the warning the ocean is giving you.

Rip Currents

Unlike longshore currents, which hug the shoreline, rip currents veer away from the shore and flow toward the horizon. They rarely flow exactly straight away from the shore, but instead travel seaward at some angle to the shoreline.

Rip currents (also known as runouts or runout conditions) can carry you off never to be seen again.

Surfers have a distinct advantage over mere mortals when it comes to rip currents, though. They have a handy dandy flota-

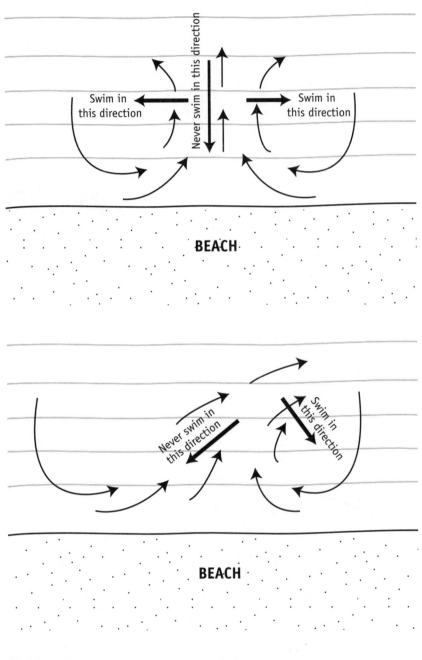

Riptides.

tion device to hang onto. One that will even take them right back to the beach, courtesy of the next wave. They have a surfboard.

The trouble comes when surfers who don't know how to surf yet get caught in a rip. Sometimes they panic and throw away their surfboards. Not a smart career move, to say the least. *Never allow yourself to become separated from your surfboard when you're being dragged toward the horizon by a rip.* Even if the board is knocking you over the head with each and every passing wave. Hang on!

So it's important to learn how to recognize a rip current.

Rip currents form as a result of a temporary imbalance in the level of the ocean. Waves pushing water shoreward at point A will cause a rip current to develop at point B.

This can happen in two ways. The first results from the beach and bottom profiles. Shorelines with projecting headlands and receding embayments refract waves; these waves tend to arrive larger at certain places than they do at others. The same effect can also be caused by offshore reefs that you can't see. The larger waves coming into a specific area will generate rip currents in their immediate surroundings. Rips caused by this kind of setup are more benign than the ones I'll talk about later on in this section. Rips caused by the geography of a given shoreline have the good grace to stay put. So long as the swell size and direction remain the same, the rips that get generated will remain the same, too.

Look for these kinds of rips in channels and other areas where the waves aren't breaking. Especially if there's an area where the waves are hammering along at a good size right next to a calm channel.

Look closely at the water. If there's a rip, the water will have a more jumbled, disorganized appearance than it will elsewhere. Do this on a day when the wind is offshore. The offshore wind will brush the surface of the water to a smooth, velvety texture.

Where the velvety texture is disrupted by an area of disorganized ripples and little choppy wavelets, that's where the rip is. If you try to spot this difference when the wind is onshore, you're not likely to see anything. The choppiness and disorganization caused by the onshore wind are going to mask any further chop or disorganization caused by the rip. Later on, when your eyes are trained at this sort of thing, you'll be able to spot rips in any kind of wind.

But not all rips are so good natured as to make their presence easily known. On days when the surf is smaller, or at places where the geography doesn't lend itself so well to the creation of a rip, rips can poot along at half power and remain surprisingly invisible to untrained eyes. But don't underestimate the power of rips that aren't fully developed. You won't get dragged off quite as fast, but you'll still get dragged off if you're not paying attention.

Rips can be very subtle. If a disorganized look isn't visible on the water, check for streaks of foam that seem to be lying on the water in areas where there aren't any waves breaking. Another sign of a rip current is weed lines—streaks of debris in the water. Little floating bits of grass, seaweed, Dixie cups, and what have you that glom together into a kind of streak of junk out on the water.

Sometimes, though, the water's just easing along wherever it wants to go and not being very demonstrative about it. Conditions like this—a broad, smooth flow of water—aren't likely to do anything to you, however. Which is good. It's when the water grabs at you from out of a place where it's not moving around or doing much of anything that you can get in trouble.

The second type of rip can occur along beaches that run straight and level for miles and miles without any sort of geographical variation. This covers just about everywhere, from

Brownsville, Texas, to Montauk Point, New York. And many other places all over the world where there's a stretch of straight, sandy beach.

Sandy beaches are never quite perfectly straight and true. There's always a bit of a trough somewhere, or a low spot in the sandbar, even if it's too slight for you to see when you're walking right through the middle of it. When a set of waves comes in along the length of beach, it pushes water into the trough. Even if the total vertical extent of the trough is measured in mere inches, the water has got to go somewhere. And if the water doesn't find a low area, it'll *make* a low area (again, mere inches of depth are all that's required) in the sandbar and push its way back out to sea in the form of a rip current. With each set of waves, the trough and sandbar will be scoured or filled at the whim of wave and tide. So the places where the rips develop aren't static. They can move up and down the shoreline.

Rips will develop, last a while, and then disappear. Or move down the beach. Or merge with other rips.

The equilibrium between waves and shoreline is dynamic. The only constant is change. Rip currents are born, exist for a time, and die. Like little puffy clouds on a sunny day.

Waves have finite dimensions—side to side as well as top to bottom. Waves coming in right in front of you extend only so far down the beach before they fade into nonexistence. Sets of waves may arrive at any given stretch of coastline in purely random fashion. And if you know how "random" really works, you won't be surprised to learn that sets of waves can repeatedly arrive at one section of beach while a neighboring section remains quiet, at least for a time. Like tossing a coin and getting a string of heads, things will eventually even out, but for a while one result is favored over another. When sets of waves occur like this, rip currents are generated in the areas where the repeated sets of waves push more water toward the beach than would otherwise happen. These rips will form and persist for as long as the water is being pushed. If enough time elapses before the waves subside, a new trough can be gouged into the sandbar by the action of the rip current. Sand is a fluid. It just flows more slowly than the water that's pushing it.

The fact that rip currents can pop up out of nowhere along sandy beaches is what kills people. Spotting rips on straight, sandy beaches where their location may shift isn't easy. Worse still, along sandy beaches rips don't always extend out beyond the line of whitewater breakers. A rip can fade back into the turbulence where the waves are breaking.

For spotting rips along sandy beaches, the same rules of recognition that apply to spotting rips caused by geography apply. But with waves coming in all over the place, it's a lot harder to do. Look for a disorganized stretch of water. Sometimes the presence of a rip will be betrayed by an area of discolored water: Rips are usually a bit murkier than the undisturbed water they're penetrating. But not always.

Also bear in mind the fact that even though there wasn't a rip to be found when you arrived at the beach and set up shop, there's nothing to prevent one from being born out of nothing, right where you or your mother or children are happily splishing around in the water.

So what are you supposed to do if you get caught in one? Not much, actually. If you suddenly notice yourself being pulled slowly away from the beach, and into deeper water, *don't panic.* What makes rip currents so dangerous is not the current itself, but that people fight them and become exhausted. That's when there's risk of drowning.

Let the rip take you for whatever ride it wants to take you for. And believe me, it won't be an "E Ticket" ride. It'll be pretty dull and boring. Rips *all* fizzle out sooner or later. If you don't do *anything* at all, you still won't be going anywhere. Maybe down the beach and out a little way, but that's it.

Just swim along with the rip until it loses interest in you. Then head to shore. Or swim with the rip at an angle that causes you to angle toward shore—being sure to go along in the general direction the rip's pulling you in. And don't swim very hard. Take it easy. Save your energy. Bob around. Admire the color of the sky or something else to make the time pass. What's the big hurry, anyway?

Getting into the Water

Walking Out

So this is it. You're down at the beach with gear in hand. You've got your nongreasy sunscreen on. Your hat and sunglasses are safely

Let's go surfing!

(photo credit: James MacLaren)

locked in the car. Your bar of surfwax is in the pocket of your surf trunks, if you're wearing them. You've got a long surfboard with a cord attached. The beach is sandy with a gentle slope out under the water. And there are 2-foot waves easing shoreward. All the elements are in place.

Walk down to the water's edge and place the cuff of your cord around your right ankle if you're right-handed, left ankle if you're left-handed. The foot with the cord will be your rear foot.

Pick up the board in the middle and carry it under your arm as you enter the ocean. Be careful to keep the nose of the board pointed straight out to sea. If it turns sideways it might get caught by a passing wave and knock you down. You don't want to embarrass yourself just yet. There'll be plenty of time for that later.

Walk out to where the water is knee deep to waist deep, being careful to keep the waves from grabbing the board as they pass by. If the waves are coming up and hitting the board while it hangs there under your arm, then turn the board so that it's

Pushing the board through whitewater.

Lifting the board over whitewater.

upright,
with the deck up and the fin(s) down. Be
sure to keep it pointed directly into where the waves are coming from. Either lay it on top of the water, pushing it through the

waves as they come at you, or hold it up above the waves, letting them pass below the board. Pay attention to your board; you'd be utterly amazed at the force with which even tiny little waves can take hold of it and smash it against you. Also, *never* turn your back to the oncoming waves.

As you walk out to where the water's knee to waist deep, notice how much time elapses between each passing wave. On some days the waves come one right after another in quick succession; on other days they're spaced well apart, a bit of time passing between each. The interval between oncoming waves will be important for what you'll be doing very soon. Take note of it.

If the waves are *real* little, be sure not to walk out past where they're breaking. For now, all you want to be dealing with is whitewater. Forget any unbroken waves. If you have to, move closer to the beach to ensure that you're dealing only with waves that have already broken.

You're now ready to position yourself to catch that first wave.

Getting Positioned

If you did it correctly, you kept the board aimed directly into the waves as you walked it out into the water. Soon you'll need to turn the board around to face the opposite direction, with the nose pointing toward the beach, so that you can catch and ride a wave.

A cautionary note: There can be a second or two between these two main orientations of the surfboard wherein the board will be *sideways* to the oncoming surf. This is a dangerous window of opportunity for mishap.

Never allow a sideways board to get between you and an oncoming, breaking or broken (whitewater) wave!

Never, ever do this!

If you find yourself looking over your sideways board at oncoming whitewater with the wave rapidly approaching, *get out of the way*. Fast! Duck down underwater and stay there until the wave passes. Or jump away to one side. But don't just grab onto the board and wrassle with it in a vain attempt to align it properly. If there's the slightest doubt in your mind as to whether or not you've got enough time to get the board properly oriented, bail out!

Why the concern? A sideways board, caught just so by even a little bitty whitewater, will connect with you at car-crash energy-release levels. This is no exaggeration. And worse still, it's usually your head (since it's often the only part of you above water) that takes the square hit. Getting knocked-out teeth, a broken nose, or a busted cheekbone is not an unlikely result.

And no, you aren't allowed to drag the board fin first out into the water in an attempt to avoid having to turn it all the way around when a wave you want to ride comes along. With the fin leading into the oncoming waves, the board is likely to get grabbed by a wave and turned sideways to bash the hell out of you.

So there you are, out in the knee- to waist-deep water with the board pointed toward the far horizon. Having just gone through a wave, you can see another one stacking up, coming your way. Now's your chance.

If you were doing it right, you were paying attention to the interval between each wave as you walked out, so you know how much time you've got to swing the board around so that it's pointing toward the beach.

Here's how you turn the board: Grab it with both hands. One hand on each side, in the middle of the board. Then swing the nose around till it points to the beach. If the fin in the water impedes your motion, just lift the board up out of the water till the fin's clear, then swing it on around. It shouldn't take more than a couple of seconds to turn the board around. It's a good idea to practice this move with your board down at the lake where

Swinging the board around

there aren't any waves. Or even on the beach before you enter the water. Never mind what the neighbors think.

Now you're in position. You've walked out to the correct depth (knee to waist deep) and successfully turned the board around.

You're now ready to take the next step. You're going to catch a wave.

Jumping Into Your Very First Wave

Despite the fact that surfers *paddle* into waves, as a beginner you'll do things differently. Paddling is a whole degree higher in difficulty and frustration and will be covered later, beginning on page 66. You're not going to paddle. You're going to jump. And it's not going to be much of a jump—more of a flop, really.

With the board pointed directly at the beach, and while holding it with both hands, one on each side, in the middle of the board, watch for whitewater that's approaching you from the rear.

Just before the wave catches you from behind, give the board a shove in the direction of the beach. At the same time, jump up and land on the board so that you're *lying down* on it. *Don't attempt to stand up.* That'll come later. For now, just flop down on the board and lie on your belly.

If you do this correctly you'll find yourself whizzing along at what seems to be breakneck speed (it isn't, really) headed straight for the beach to the accompaniment of loud cheers from your friends and family. The sight of a good friend or family member catching her first wave invariably causes the folks watching from the beach to respond with vigor.

Unfortunately, your odds of doing this correctly on the first try are pretty lousy. More likely, you're going to take some kind of awkward and hilarious spill. It takes time and practice to learn to jump into waves successfully (bit it's still much quicker and easier than learning to *paddle* for waves).

If you jump on the board a bit too far forward, the nose will dip beneath the surface of the water (this is called *pearling,* in surfing lingo, and it's a verb). The board will instantly dive for the bottom, bringing all forward motion to an abrupt halt. You'll be thrown off the front of the board head first. The board, being buoyant, will pop up into the air at about the same time that you pop back up for air. When you pearl on takeoff remember to *stay down underwater* for a while to give the board time to come crashing back down. You're safe from it underwater. Sometimes, not often, however, the board will get slingshotted back down at you in the water via the action of your cord with murderous energy. So be careful if you pearl.

Her board is completely underwater in a deep pearl—this ride is over.

If you jump on the board a bit too far to the rear, the nose will stick way up in the air. With the board at such an extreme angle to the surface of the water, there's no way for it to plane across the water. It bogs down and stops immediately, and the wave continues along to the beach without you.

If you jump on the board too far to either side, you'll simply roll off the board as it tips over. If you hang on for dear life in this situation, you'll find yourself being dragged through the water, getting firehosed in the face, with the board tipped completely up on one edge. Or even rolling all the way over, upside down. So let go of the board should you tip to either side.

You might think that jumping on the board so that your body is nicely aligned with it wouldn't be difficult. But it's amazingly easy to land on the board with your body at an angle to the centerline of the board. Trying to correct your angle on the board isn't easy. As you wriggle and squirm to align yourself properly, just about anything can happen. Except your actually regaining a modicum of sensible control, of course.

Sometimes you get it almost completely right, except that the board's not pointed directly toward the beach. In these situations the tendency is to want to lean toward the side of the board that's away from the wave, in an attempt to steer the board onto a straighter course. If you were standing on the board this would be just the thing to do. But since you're lying down, riding a tiny little whitewater wave, the edge of the board away from the wave generally dips below the surface of the water and you get caught in a weird sideways pearling action where the board progressively tips over at the same time that it gets more and more sideways to the wave. This can end in any number of climactic and hilarious ways, depending on the exact orientation of the board, the wave you're riding, and the extent to which you fail to release your death grip on the board, prolonging the action.

The timing of your jump into the wave is critical. Jump too late and the wave simply knocks you off the board as you attempt to get situated on it. That, or nothing happens at all:

The wave just passes you by. Jump too soon and the wave encounters you as a *stationary* target. The sudden impact of the wave smashing into you from behind will probably knock you right off the board. Should you manage to hang on, nothing much happens. The wave passes you by. Practice is the only thing that will help you get your jump right.

Here's how you'd *like* it to happen. You want to jump up on the deck of the board so that you're aligned with your head and feet in the same direction as the centerline of the board. You also want to be centered directly over the middle of the board, the centerline. And you want to be situated so that the nose of the board is as close as it can be to the water without actually dipping below the surface. The first half of this equation—being properly aligned on the surfboard—takes practice, but isn't difficult to learn. The second half—getting the nose of the board to lie just above, but not under, the water—is trickier. No two surfboards are quite alike in this respect, so there's no well-marked spot on which you can just plant yourself down and expect to avoid pearling or bogging down. Trial and error will teach you where you need to be on any given board. Some people can instantly and accurately gauge where they ought to be lying on the board. Other folks aren't so lucky, and they've just got to put in the time until things start to feel right. Everybody eventually figures it out. If you're having trouble here, just be persistent. You'll get the hang of it.

Proning It Out

So now you're lying in a prone position on the board and you're actually riding a wave to the beach! Now what? For now, it's more than enough to merely lie on the board, still gripping it with both hands, and glide to the beach until the fin drags in the sand and you come to a stop. Do this until you can do it *every single time* without wiping out.

When you've gotten to the point where proning it out is a snap, you'll also have gotten to a point where you're starting to understand the nuances and subtleties of how waves act upon you and your surfboard. You already know more than you think you know. But don't get cocky: The next level, learning to stand up, is *quite* a step up.

There's an intermediate phase between proning it out and standing up, which people don't take the time to do. But they should. This phase really helps teach you how to keep your balance when you're on your feet.

As you're proning along, *come to your knees.* Try to ride waves in a kneeling position. You can still hold onto the sides of the board with your hands, but you'll get a taste of what it feels like to have to maintain balance with your center of mass raised off the board. After you've successfully mastered the basic move of coming in on your knees, *take your hands off the board* and do it. This teaches you (in the most benign way possible) to use your arms and body to maintain balance on top of the board while riding a wave.

Proning it out.

If you get good at riding in a kneeling position before you make your first attempt to stand up, you'll find standing to be a lot easier than if you jump directly from proning it out to standing up, with nothing in between.

Attempting to Stand Up

Onward and upward. Remember when you did something called a "squat thrust" in PE class? It's a deep knee bend where you put your hands on the ground and kick your legs out behind you into a push-up position, then reverse the movement and return to your feet. Well, coming to your feet on a surfboard is very similar to the second half of a squat thrust, the part where

She's riding on her knees, hands gripping the sides of the board.

She's riding on her knees, hands off the sides of the board.

you pull your legs back underneath yourself and come to an upright position.

As you're riding along in prone position, get a good grip on the sides of the surfboard with your hands and then do a kind of push-up, with your entire torso up off of the board. As soon as your body's clear of the board, jerk your legs up and under yourself, with your knees completely bent and your feet as far beneath you as you can get 'em. Then stand up. Easy, right? Well, maybe not, but in order to stand up, you *have* to learn to do this. The trick is to do it as quickly as possible. Bang! and you're on your feet.

For now, it's okay for you to flounder around while getting to your feet. You're in close, right next to the beach. And you're riding a piddly little whitewater that's going to fizzle out on the sand in short order. If you get up, flail around, and go *splat* into the water, it's no big deal. Just grab the board, run out to the waist-deep water, and do it again.

If you're one of the lucky ones, it'll come easy. For the rest of you, don't fret. The practice and repetition are doing you a world of good whether or not you notice anything good happening. I'll discuss standing up in much greater detail beginning on page 83.

If you followed my advice and got a longboard, you'll be glad now. Longboards are much more forgiving of the control errors made by beginners, and you'll need all the help you can get when it comes to learning how to stand up on a surfboard.

When you get the hang of standing up while close to shore in the shallow water, don't be in a hurry to start steering the board. Right now you're traveling too slowly on the waves you're riding to perform deliberate control maneuvers. That'll happen later, when you're farther along, and farther out on bigger waves, and traveling faster. In order to get out there you'll have to learn how to paddle.

Learn to Surf

1.

Coming to your feet.

2.

3.

4.

Learning to Paddle

Chances are by the time you've done all the above you've done a fair amount of paddling around, too. But even if you *have* done a bit of paddling by now, you haven't done it very well. Not unless you're some kind of natural talent.

The reasons for waiting before learning to paddle are twofold. First, without proper motivation, something as difficult as paddling can be a complete turnoff. Second, after you've ridden a wave or two you're clued in like an expert on what having the nose of the board a little too low or a little too high can do to the board's performance. This critical business of having the nose of the board *just above* the water applies to your paddling as well.

To begin, get out in the water where there are no waves breaking. Dealing with whitewater makes learning to paddle a difficult, if not impossible, task. If the waves are tiny, walk the board out past where they're breaking and then have at it. If the waves are bigger, try to find a trough or dead spot where they glurp down into oblivion, and learn to paddle around in there. That, or wait for a day when the waves have subsided to the point where you can walk out past them.

Now climb up on top of the board.

Lie down on it exactly the same way you did to ride those piddly little whitewaters.

Align yourself so that you're centered over the centerline of the board. Now adjust yourself so that the nose of the board is *just above* the surface of the water. Almost touching, but not quite. Try to remember where you are on the board and what it feels like. This is the position you'll always be in when paddling.

Now, paddle. Use a plain, overhand stroke. The same stroke you use when swimming, first one arm, then the other. Don't pull your arms way up out of the water when bringing them around in front of you. Lift them just barely out of the water. But be sure not to drag your hands through or along the water. Just get them clear of the water, then bring them forward and down into the water for the power stroke. Power stroke back, and repeat. Some people like to do their power stroke with a downward motion; others like to take the power stroke out to the side. You do whatever feels most comfortable, whatever's least tiring.

If you're situated on top of the board correctly, it'll plane across the water, making it much easier to paddle. Mind you, not easy—just easier. Paddling is hard work no matter how you cut it. To actually get anywhere, you've got to burn some energy.

There are no shortcuts in paddling, but there *are* long cuts.

If you're lying on the board wrong, paddling becomes nearly impossible. You'll flail away but nothing will happen.

Most people tend to lie on the board so that its nose sticks way up in the air, out of the water. The board no longer

Good paddling technique. Note that the nose of the board is *just above* the water.

planes across the water but instead plows through it. With the board plowing water this way, you're not going to go anywhere. If things as powerful as waves don't have enough energy to keep a board moving when you've got its nose way up in the air, you certainly don't either.

Some people tend to lie on the board so that its nose keeps going under. If you do this, the result will be a fresh faceful of water with each stroke of your arms—and you won't go anywhere.

If you're doing things right you can take a few strokes to get the board moving, then stop paddling and pull your arms up out of the water, and the board will continue on all by itself for a little while. This assumes you are on a longboard, of course. A shortboard will stop dead the instant you quit stroking, and so will a bodyboard.

Bad paddling technique—he's too far back and the nose is too far out of the water.

Bad paddling technique—he's too far forward and the nose is underwater, going down deeper with each paddling stroke.

Paddling Through Whitewater

To get out past where the breakers are you've obviously got to go *through* the breakers to get there. You'll need to learn to paddle out through oncoming whitewater.

This is serious physical labor. If you're out of shape you'll find out when paddling out through the breakers.

Practice on a day with waves of less than 3 feet. With waves any bigger than that you have no chance at all of succeeding. None. I don't care if you're Charles Atlas and Jack LaLanne rolled into one, you're not going anywhere if the waves are bigger than 3 feet. That is, unless you get stupendously lucky and hit a lull in the waves that lasts for about 15 minutes. And even if you do manage to squeak all the way out on a day with waves that are larger than 3 feet, you still have a problem. You're faced with attempting to catch and ride waves that are too big for you. It's possible to get into real trouble on larger waves. Hold off for now.

Waves come in *sets* and *lulls*. The ocean tosses surf at you for a while, then it takes a break before tossing more waves at you. Waves come in groups that are called sets. Between the groups are periods of time with no waves or smaller waves. These periods of time with less wave activity are called lulls.

A lull is your best bet for paddling out successfully. So teach yourself to look for, and recognize, lulls. Like everything else, it takes practice.

Here's how to paddle out through whitewater: As a wall of it approaches take a couple of extra-strong paddling strokes, to build up a little momentum to use against the wave. Just before the wave hits you, grab the sides of the board—with both hands—near your shoulders. Be sure to have the board pointed *exactly* into the wave. When the wave hits just hold on as tight as you can and wait for it to pass behind you. If you've done everything correctly your board will still be pointed directly out to sea, you'll still be on top of it, centered where you ought to be, and you can resume paddling in time for the *next* wall of whitewater that's coming your way.

Here's what can go wrong: If the board is angled off to one side or the other, the whitewater will grab it and spin you right around, pulling you and the board shoreward as it does so. You can wind up with the board pointed toward shore after one of these. Or sideways. Or upside down. Or any combination of these.

If the nose of the board is a trifle too far up out of the water, the whitewater will get under it and flip the whole board up and over, backward, with such force and vigor that you might bang your jaw into its deck.

If the nose is too low, the whitewater will get a good grip on the board and yank it out from under you, knocking it well back toward the beach.

Paddling out through a whitewater.

To successfully push yourself through a whitewater takes a particular combination of brute force, a deft sense of balance, and lightning reflexes. Nothing else that you might have done or might ever do will call upon these elements in quite the same way. There's no pool of useful knowledge that you can draw upon to assist you in paddling your board through whitewater. Again, practice, practice, practice.

You'll quickly discover that whitewater varies in strength, speed, and degree of turbulence. Pay attention to these characteristics. After you've learned to spot the differences, you can begin to exploit them.

Weak, petered-out whitewater can sometimes be gotten through with the following technique: Just as the whitewater is about to hit you, do a push-up maneuver by grabbing the board directly beneath your shoulders and extending your arms fully. With your torso up and away from the board, the whitewater can churn safely below you with nothing to grab hold of and jerk around.

Sometimes you can go up and over an oncoming whitewater by doing the following: Just before the whitewater gets to you, sit back on the board for an instant, to get the nose to come up out of the water high enough so that it's about even with the top of the arriving whitewater. At the exact instant that the wave hits you, you need to have jumped forward on the board and grasped it way up by the nose with your hands in a death grip on both sides. Needless to say, this must be timed just right. Too late, and you're hurtling over backward toward the shore. Too soon, and you're buried under a violently churning mass of whitewater, getting the board wrenched from your grip.

You can go *under* larger whitewater. There's two ways to do it. The first method is called turning turtle. As the whitewater approaches, roll the board completely upside down and get yourself underneath it, holding onto the sides for dear life. The other way is to hop off the side and slide the board under your arm to where you can reach all the way across the deck, up near the nose, and grab the far side with one hand while holding the near side with the other. Just as the whitewater hits you, duck your head and hang on for dear life. Done correctly, the whitewater will pass overhead, leaving you to clamber back up on top of the surfboard, paddle like hell for a bit, and gird your loins for battle with the *next* whitewater.

If you have a small surfboard you can also go under a whitewater by coming to a hands-and-knees position on the board just before the whitewater hits. Coming up off the board that way causes it to momentarily sink down underwater. Timing here is critical. *Just* as the whitewater reaches you, fall back to a prone position on your (momentarily) submerged board. Hang on tight and you'll pop right out of the back of the wave. This is a dicey move. It's not recommended for beginners and is impossible on a longboard.

Turning turtle.

Sometimes the whitewater is more than you can handle no matter what. In that case, your job is to successfully identify these too-powerful whitewaters—and avoid them.

Waves that crash over with a tube (you really don't have any business out there in surf like this yet, but people do make mistakes) produce a particularly explosive whitewater. Boom! You're not going to make it through something like this. If you see a situation developing ahead of you where the wave looks like it's going to come over with a real bang, hang back. Don't even bother to paddle. If you paddle like hell to meet an exploding whitewater, it's going to nail you. So rest up. Sit there. Let the whitewater simmer down as it travels toward you. Go over it using the techniques discussed above and turn your attention to the next wave.

Holding the board near the nose to go through a whitewater.

Deciding on whether to approach a wave or hang back takes experience. The only way you're going to get experience is to paddle out and *have* the experiences. Some days will be better than others, but the rewards of surfing will always outweigh the difficulties.

Waves that break directly on top of you are another thing altogether. You could get hurt. I burst an eardrum one time when a wave broke directly on top of me.

If a wave looks like it might break right on top of you, bail out. *Get off the board.* Over the side and down deep. And stay there until the wave passes over you.

Sitting Up on the Board

After you've arrived at the place out past the breakers where you'll wait to catch a wave, you'll need to be sitting up on your board. Lying on the board can get tiresome. More important, as you lie there, your head down on the deck of the board, your range of vision is extremely limited. You can't see the waves coming. Therefore, you need to learn to sit up on the board.

To sit up from a prone position, you need to grab the sides of the board with your hands and push your torso away from it. As you sit up, scoot your butt forward a bit, so that when you're done you'll have the board dead level with the water or with the nose a touch on the elevated side. If you do this correctly you'll find yourself sitting on top of the board, straddling it with your legs over the sides. If it feels more stable to continue holding onto the sides of the board after you've reached a sitting position, then do so. Expect to go over the side when you try to sit up on the board the first few times. A surfboard is about the only thing in the world that's tippier than a canoe. Stay with it, you'll get the hang of it sooner or later.

Turning the Board Around from a Sitting Position

Once seated out past the breakers, you'll need to know how to change direction. The reason is that to watch for oncoming waves, you must face the far horizon. But to catch those waves, you must face the shore. A direction change is necessary to get from one orientation to the other. And unless the direction change is done quickly, you'll never have time to get reoriented and catch a wave before it passes you by. Therefore, you must learn to pivot the board around from a sitting position.

From the sitting position, grab the sides of the board with your hands and scoot back until the nose of the board rises up out of the water. Don't place your weight *too* far back or you might wind up toppling all the way over backward. With your weight to the rear and the nose of the board up in the air, pull with your hand on the side of the board that's closest to the new direction you want to aim for. Let go with the other hand and just yank on the board. The nose will instantly pivot around. As it drops down to the level of the water, be sure to readjust your position on the board to relevel it. Otherwise you'll go over the side. As the nose comes down into the water and you've resituated yourself to keep the board level, grab the sides with both hands again and scoot forward to keep the nose from heading skyward once more.

You can also drop immediately into a prone paddling position upon completing a pivot. If you're pressed for time (with a wave rapidly approaching), just lie back down on the board and start paddling for the wave right away.

Incorrect pivot—pushing the board around.

Correct pivot—pulling the board around.

Be sure to recenter yourself over the board as described earlier (page 66).

Pivoting is difficult but you have to pivot for a reason: It's quick. Much quicker than lying there on the board and attempting to *swim* it around to where you want it pointed. Swimming the board around is what beginners seem to want to do in every single case, but it simply takes more time than you have before the wave you want to catch arrives. When you swim the board around, the wave will catch you halfway through the maneuver, with the board in the dreaded *sideways* orientation.

A successful pivot will allow you to reorient the board in plenty of time to work up a good head of steam as you paddle to catch a wave.

Paddling For Whitewater

Let's go surfing.

We're going to start out by paddling for whitewater waves. They're a whole lot easier to catch than waves that haven't broken yet. The ride's a bit dull, though.

Paddle out into the middle of where the waves are breaking. Don't bother paddling all the way out past where they're breaking, though. That's too far. Just get out there in the middle of all that whitewater. Then wait for a momentary lull in the action.

You're going to need a little breather to rest up before attempting to catch a wave by paddling instead of jumping into it like we did a while back (page 57). You're also going to need a bit of time to pivot the board around and get it pointed straight at the beach in the proper orientation for catching a wave. Watch for the waves coming your way to ease off a bit.

So, there you sit in the middle of a lull and here comes a set of waves stacking up outside, on their way in. What you do next is really a matter of common sense, but since it seems to elude many beginners, here's a blow-by-blow description:

As the set approaches assay the looks of things, to assure yourself that the wave you want isn't going to break right on top of you. Look for any other surfers coming your way, already riding the wave. These folks have the right-of-way, every time. Wait to catch another wave if there's somebody coming your way on the one you picked. Otherwise you just might get run over. Surfers are quite territorial about waves they've already caught. Let them have their waves.

If the approaching wave looks suitably small and safe, make your move. Pivot the board around (go back to page 75 and read this move again if you've forgotten it) so that you're facing the beach. As the wave approaches, start paddling with all your might: a full sprint paddle. Do this in time to build up a good head of steam before the whitewater hits you—but not so soon that you'll be worn out from that sprint paddle when the wave makes it to you. Just as the wave hits you, quit paddling and grab both sides of the board with your hands. Wherever it feels most comfortable. Done right, as the wave jolts you hard from behind, you'll accelerate from 0 to 60 in about half a second and be riding the wave in a prone position. When you regain a bit of stability, stand up.

That's all there is to it.

Needless to say, anything and everything can and will go wrong while you're trying this. You'll get beat and battered in more ways than you'd have thought possible. Since you're farther out, away from the beach, be extra sure that your cord's properly attached to both yourself and your surfboard. Avoid going out farther than you'd be able to swim, just in case you do get separated from your board.

Up and riding.

Paddling For Waves Before They Break

So by now you've learned to walk the board out into the ocean, turn it around, jump on board; you've ridden the waves lying prone and on your knees; you've learned to stand, to paddle, and to pivot the board.

Now for the main event. *Real surfing.* You've done just about everything possible preliminary to actually catching an unbroken wave, the thing that real surfers catch.

This time, paddle all the way out past the breakers. If there are other surfers out in the water, paddle to where they're sitting around waiting for the next wave. Be careful to stay out of everybody's way. Remember, as a beginner you're the least-experienced surfer out there. Try to be courteous and respectful. The other surfers might get nasty if you don't.

If there are no other surfers around get *just past,* but no farther than, where the whitewater starts breaking.

If you paddle too far out, you'll never catch anything. If you paddle just short of where you ought to be, waves will break on top of you. It's a fine line. And as with every element of surfing, getting it right takes practice. Big waves break farther out, little ones break closer in. You need to watch, make judgment calls, and hope for the best.

One nice thing about being out past the last of the breakers is that the waves aren't clobbering you anymore as you sit and wait for a nice one. It's real peaceful out there. Stop a minute and take in the scenery. This is one of the reasons that you wanted to learn to surf in the first place.

Your goal now is to time things so that you're paddling for a wave just before it breaks, but not so close to that point of breaking that you won't have time to jump to your feet as soon as you feel the wave lift and accelerate you.

It's dicey. Scan the waves coming your way. Get a sense of what they look like before they break, and of how long it takes for a wave to first rise up, then topple over. Compare that time with how long it takes you to get to a standing position on your board. Yark! Got to learn to get on your feet even faster. Pay heed to your fellow surfers. Get familiar with the sorts of waves they paddle for and the sorts they leave alone. Emulate them.

If you attempt to catch a wave too soon, before it breaks . . . exactly nothing happens. Quite forgiving, in a way. You paddle like hell, the wave travels under you, lifts you, and then lets you back down as it continues on toward the beach without you. Don't despair and don't get frustrated and rush the next one. The impulse at this point is to catch one too close to breaking. Several things can happen here. None of them good.

The wave might crash directly on top of you as you lie on the board paddling. Depending on the wave and your exact relation to it, you may merely be washed off the board, or perhaps get your face smashed into its deck. You may also be hit by your board.

If the wave doesn't get you before you start to your feet, there's still plenty of time and ways for things to go south after you're up. Here are a few.

⊃ Whether standing, prone, or in an intermediate position, you can plummet to the bottom of the wave where the nose of your board will bury itself into the water in the mother of all pearls.

⊃ You can just make it to your feet and then have the force of the breaking wave knock you all over the place.

⊃ You can hit somebody else who's paddling out.

⊃ You can hit somebody else who's riding the wave.

Try your dead-level best to hit that happy medium wherein you manage to catch the wave but not so late that it's going to do you bodily harm.

Once again, there's no substitute for practice, practice, practice.

One way to increase your odds of success is to be a ferocious paddler. The harder you can paddle, the farther out you can catch waves before they break.

Butterfly paddling stroke. The surfer is in the middle of a *backoff*.

Paddle for unbroken waves butterfly-style, with both arms at the same time, instead of using the crawl stroke that got you out to where the waves are breaking. The butterfly stroke is more powerful and causes you to accelerate faster. But it's exhausting, so don't use it for anything except catching a wave.

If *at any point* somebody near you whistles, shouts, or otherwise makes her presence known, *stop paddling.* Give the wave away.

You're not yet at the point where you can assess subtleties of right-of-way, so you must assume that anybody at all making a fuss is doing so for a good reason. Yield the right-of-way. Even when you don't know what the right-of-way is. There'll be another wave later on. Catch that one instead.

Since the business of coming to your feet is so critical, it's time to go into detail.

Standing Up for Real

In the beginning, when you were learning to jump into little dribblers in waist-deep water, it was smartest just to get to your feet the best way you knew how. You weren't ready to handle a proper stance back then. Now the time has come to address this vital aspect of surfing.

Standing up involves having a *stance.* And on a surfboard, not just any old stance will do. Gotta have the *right* stance. And you've got to be able to just *jump* into that stance without any forethought. Bing! and you're up.

To begin with, you must stand centered over the centerline of the board. Nowhere else will do. Practice this at home. Lay the board down, making sure to push the fin down into the dirt, or take it out of the board (some are removable), so you won't break it off as you stand on top of the board. Now stand on the center of the board. Not front-to-back center, but the side-to-side center.

Front-to-back positioning is determined solely by what it takes to keep the nose of the board just above the water. No two surfboards respond quite the same in this regard, and you'll just have to work it out for yourself. Keep in mind, of course, that if you're too far forward, the nose dips below the water and everything comes to a screeching halt as you pearl, and if you're too far back you'll bog down and stop. It will all become self-evident when you ride a wave.

Now that you know what part of the board you should be standing on, you need to know where each foot should be planted.

When you stand on a surfboard, you stand crosswise to your direction of travel. Your direction of travel is wherever the nose of the board is pointed. In general, right-handed people face to the right of their direction of travel, and left-handed people face to the left. If the nose of the board is 12 o'clock, right-handers face somewhere around 1 or 2 o'clock. Left-handers face 10 or 11. But if this feels the slightest bit uncomfortable or awkward, and the other way around feels more natural, then by all means stand the way that feels most comfortable. I'll continue on as if all you right-handers and left-handers are standing as you're "supposed to," but if you're different, then factor that into these instructions.

If you're right-handed, your right foot (or, in surfer parlance, regular foot) will be your back foot. For left-handers, the left foot will be your back foot. Your back foot is your *power* foot. It's the foot that'll be carrying most of your weight. It's also the foot with which you'll be applying most of the twisting and torquing forces that maneuver the board. If your back foot's placed incorrectly, there's nothing in the world that your front foot can do to rectify the problem.

Your back foot should be planted a hair over the board's centerline toward the side of the board that your toes point toward—no more than an inch or so off center. Your heel will be closer to the centerline than your toes. Stop right now and go over to the board and put your foot where I just told you to put it. If you're a right-hander, your back foot will point to 2 o'clock.

Reverse this if you're a lefty (or, goofy-footed) and point the foot to 10 o'clock.

Your front foot should be planted with its toes just about on the centerline of the board or maybe a little across it. The toes of your front foot will be closer to the centerline of the board than the heel. And for righties, the front foot points to 1 o'clock. Lefties, 11.

Your heels will be closer together than your toes.

Try this on your surfboard in your backyard or living room, with book in hand.

This is your stance. Or pretty close to it. *Not everybody stands on a surfboard exactly the same way.* If this feels a bit awkward, adjust. But not too much. Your stance is the way it is because that's the way it *has* to be to control your surfboard.

Regular foot   Goofy foot

Correctly positioned, you'll be centered over the board with an open-toed stance. You'll either face to the right or to the left of the direction you'll be traveling in, depending on which foot you place forward. You'll be controlling the board by applying weight to the toes (or, rather, balls) or heels of one or both feet. Heel and toe weighting and unweighting, coupled with a twisting action of your entire body, are all you've got to control the board, so pay careful attention to your stance. Be sure to get it right.

Never stand up with your feet straddling the centerline of the board and pointed directly at the nose.

That's called a parallel stance. Experts use it occasionally just to display their mastery of surfing and a reckless disregard for life, limb, and any future offspring. The board *will* come up sideways between your legs. I'll leave it up to your imagination as to what happens after that.

Learn your stance. Learn it well. And be able to leap into it in the blink of an eye at the very instant you catch a wave.

That instant comes when you feel yourself starting to pitch down and forward as you're paddling for a wave.

Use the burst of butterfly sprint paddling that I described earlier. As the wave comes up

Proper stance for riding straight (i.e., not turning).

and under you from behind, it lifts you. And then for the briefest of moments you hang suspended before starting back down, still out on the front of the wave. At this exact moment take one to three more good strokes. It always takes a couple of strokes more than you think it should. Beginners tend to stand up as soon as they feel themselves no longer being lifted by the wave. This is too soon. You've got to be dropping back down the face of the wave before you can stop paddling and attempt to stand up. Stand too soon and you won't catch the wave.

As soon as you begin to drop down the face of the wave, leap into your stance.

And you're surfing!

This surfer is preparing to stand up as he begins to drop down the face of the wave.

The feeling of glissading at high velocity down the slick, sparkly face of an open-ocean wave is incredibly appealing and addictive. But unless you take drastic measures, it's an extremely fleeting sensation.

You take off, stand up, head shoreward, and guess what? The wave breaks. Whitewater, again. You need to figure out a way to stay out on that surface of blue diamonds, the open wave face. Fortunately, there's a technique for doing just that. It's called angling.

Learn to angle, and you'll be a surfer.

It's that simple, but you've got to work for it. And at this stage of the game, your next step involves some tricky mental work as well as the most difficult physical requirements to date.

To learn to angle, you've got to know why you should be angling. To know why, you've got to understand the essentials of what makes a good surfing wave, as opposed to a run-of-the-mill wave.

This leads us to wave *shape*.

Wave Shape and How It Affects Your Direction of Travel

When you stroked into your first wave (as described above) you may not have noticed it, but you chose a direction of travel the instant you stood up on the board. Actually, you made your choice by not making a choice. By not choosing a direction when you stood up, the wave made that choice for you. Straight to the beach. In surfing parlance, you were surfing *straight off*.

Unbeknownst to you, there were two other choices that you could've made.

You could've gone either *right* or *left*.

In other words, you don't have to just ride straight to the beach, letting the wave break and having to put up with yet another whitewater ride. You can also angle off to the side, one way or the other, as you head shoreward.

Stop for a minute to consider this. For some, the concept is a giveaway. For most, it's very difficult to assimilate.

Consider a wave that comes to the beach as a long, long wall of water. Rather than use just that tiny little bit of the wall that going straight off to the beach allows you, you can head off at an angle, charging down the line, gobbling up as much of that sweet, sparkly wall of water as possible.

This is the essence of true surfing. No more. No less.

But in order to slice off down the line like a rifle shot, the wave you're riding must have good *shape*.

Waves, as they head toward the beach, may break in some places but not others. The ideal wave breaks in a particular spot as it approaches the shore. As the wave continues toward the beach, the area that's breaking works itself down the line or wall as the entire wave continues shoreward. With luck, this happens smoothly and evenly. Waves that do this have good shape.

When a wave comes over all at once—that is, when a long wall of water all decides to break at the same time—it's called a *closeout*.

For surfing, closeouts are no good. Unless you're at the stage before you've learned to angle down the line. In which case they're just fine. Better, even, than most spots, because there won't be a big crowd out there with you. You'll pretty much have things all to yourself.

But for long rides across slick, sparkling water, closeouts are lousy. Because even if you do know how to drive down the line, you're going to be dealing with a whitewater ride in short order. No matter where you go after taking off, the whole wave is going to come over all at once, and you're back to dealing with a whitewater. Pthhh.

A closeout will show itself as a roller in the distance, come closer, then stand up and break all along its length, turning from green, unbroken water to a frothing wall of whitewater everywhere all at the same time. Like a yardstick set on its side edge and then pushed over. The whole length of the yardstick falls over at the same time.

If the waves are closing out there's no reason to attempt to angle down the line. Nothing to gain.

So what about waves that *don't* come over all at once?

A wave with good shape will come shoreward and break in just one spot; as it continues shoreward, the area of broken whitewater will work its way progressively down the line, from one end to the other. A lot like the closing of a zipper.

Waves with good shape make you want to learn to angle.

What happens is that as you angle down the line, the wave breaks right along with you. You remain in that deliciously slick part of the wave as you ride along.

Waves that have good shape are said to *peel off.* A peeling wave lets you whistle down the line while keeping the best, most powerful, sweetest part of the wave whistling right along with you. You stay on the unbroken face but never outrace it to wind up out on the dead part of the wave, where it's hardly even standing up, let alone breaking.

For this, you've got to angle.

Angling Left or Right

There are two ways to go about angling. You can either take off at an angle, or take off straight and then do a turn that causes you to angle.

Taking off at an angle involves aiming the board a bit off to the side of straight in as you paddle to catch a wave. But don't take too radical an angle when paddling—you'll never catch the wave. The more extreme the angle, the more difficult it is to get going fast enough to slip down and into the wave. It's best to take off almost directly straight in, angling only slightly. This slight angle will usually cause you to make a slight turn and you'll wind up with a decent angle down the line, at least as long as you're *facing* the wave.

Facing the wave is called *frontside.*

Angling frontside is a snap. *Backside* is a whole different matter. It's a booger. We'll save that for later.

You've also got to learn which way to angle. As you aim toward the beach in the early stages of taking off, you can angle right or you can angle left. These immutable directions that are the same for everybody, everywhere, are determined by the shape of the wave.

For now, you need to know that a wave can peel off either right or left. Whichever way the wave goes, you want to go, too. Keep in mind that waves can lose their good shape, quit peeling, and close out at any step along the way. It's up to you to be able to tell what's going to happen ahead of time, and take appropriate measures to suit the changing aspect of the wave you're riding. This thicket of complexity drives many people to distraction and causes them to quit the sport. They just can't handle the rapid-fire sequence of events that demand an immediate, proper response. This same element of complexity is also what causes many people to become addicted to surfing. If you can handle the decision-making process, surfing is an extraordinarily satisfying activity wherein you're master of a very dynamic and untamed environment.

Now we've come to *turning* the board.

The Frontside Turn

Despite the fact that angling will vastly improve the quality of your rides on waves with good shape, not much happens when you're angling, aside from whizzing down the line.

The sensation of slicing a deep carve into the yielding face of a wave, pulling the Gs, and accelerating out of the turn to race the wave down the line is something else.

Catch the wave and jump to your feet.

As you're *dropping in* down the face of the wave, put your weight on your rear (power) foot. This will cause the nose of the board to lift into the air a bit, depending on exactly how much weight you applied to that rear foot. As soon as this effect starts to take hold, lean forward (toward 2 o'clock—10 o'clock if you're a lefty—not toward the nose of the board) out over the ball and toes of your power foot and at the same time give your whole body (it's okay to use your arms, too) a twist in the direction of the wave. If you're right-handed, with your right foot in the rear, you'll twist to your right. If you're a lefty, with your left foot to the rear, you'll twist to your left. While twisting around, readjust your weight to place a bit more than half of it on your *front* foot. Done properly, the board will swing around smartly and point down the line at a nice angle. The instant the board is aimed down the line properly, recenter your weight over the middle of the board. Bingo! You've done a frontside turn.

The frontside turn can be practiced by pretending, on solid ground. You don't even need a surfboard. Just visualize yourself weighting, twisting, reweighting, and recentering. In the space of about a second. Quick, but not too quick. Don't hurl yourself around with a pronounced jerking motion.

A large part of surfing is style. Drawing your moves out with a deceptive fluidity and grace, making it look easy by not forcing them. Mind you, you can tear up a wave yet remain extremely stylish. Check out footage of Kelly Slater in a surf movie some time, if you can't catch him in person somewhere. Amazing style coupled with no-nonsense speed, power, and force.

The idea is to develop your style along with your basic ability to merely do the moves.

Frontside turning motion.

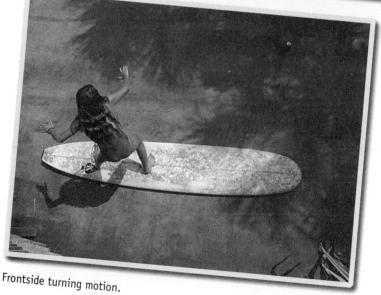

Frontside turning motion.

Down the line, in trim, going right.

The Backside Turn

This took me a year and a half to get down properly. Fortunately, you'll do a lot better than I did. I have yet to encounter *anybody* who took as long to learn a backside turn as I did.

Start out by catching the wave. Drop down and in. As with the frontside turn, you want to begin by placing extra weight over your rear (power) foot. As before, the nose comes up.

But instead of putting your weight on the ball and toes of your power foot, you're going to lean back (toward 10 o'clock—2 o'clock if you're a lefty—not toward the tail of your board) and bear down on your heel.

Your body, for whatever atavistic reasons, will resist this. Reflexes you never knew you had will kick in in an attempt to prevent you from placing your weight over the heel of your power foot. In order to surf backside, you must overcome your body's reflexive resistance.

So bear down on that heel. Then lean back and twist in the direction you want to travel. Presuming that you're a right-handed person, when you do the backside turn you're going to be going *left*. Your left foot will be your lead foot, and your right foot will be your rear, or power, foot. Coming to a standing position before turning, you'll be facing *right*.

The rotation you want to make will have your left (leading) arm swinging around toward the wave face ahead of you to your left. You'll wind up facing toward the beach with your body, placing the wave on which you're angling down the line behind you. Stop and take the time to properly digest this. It's important.

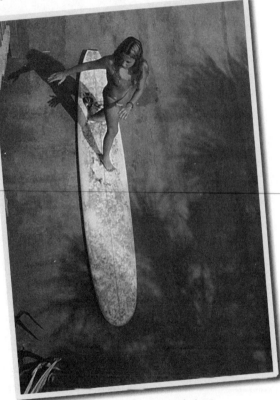

Twisting around for your backside turn.

Be sure to reverse everything if you're a lefty.

Needless to say, as you're looking down the line over your shoulder, you won't have the range of vision that you had when you were facing the wave after your frontside turn. From here on, though, things are pretty much the same as with the frontside turn. While the board comes around, angling down the line, shift your weight a touch forward and then recenter. Just like you did for the frontside turn but using a completely different set of muscles and reflexes.

A backside turn

Having just completed your backside turn, you're now surfing "backside."

Once you reach this particular plateau, where you can go left or right with equal ease, the sky's the limit. But don't plan on working out all the little details of your backside turn (or even your frontside turn) in one afternoon. You'll have to put in the time.

Once you can turn—both ways—it's time to learn how to unturn.

straightening Off and Why You Want To

I mentioned earlier that a wave that's peeling along as nice as can be might suddenly change its mind and close out. This happens all the time when you're surfing and it brings us to a new aspect of wave shape, the section.

A *section* is a place on the wave where just a portion of the wave closes out. Not the whole wave, just a chunk of it. But it's enough to call a halt to your merry angling *down the line.*

You'll discover—should you steam senselessly into a section while angling along—that this is an opportunity to take a particularly vicious type of wipeout. It won't happen every time, but once is enough for any lifetime.

What can happen is that as the churning whitewater encounters the side (remember, you're angling along here) of your board, it can flip the board up in such a way as to karate chop you with the board's side at terrific force. *This happens faster than you can believe.*

In one of these wipeouts the board can be bounced sideways by the whitewater, catch its outside edge in a sideways pearl and flip you off, bounce back into the whitewater, and then rebound off the whitewater into your exposed body with bone-breaking force, all before you have time to fall underwater out of harm's way. What this means is that you *can't* get out of the way. If it happens to take place at a more leisurely pace, your body might have sufficient time to fall into the water. Which means your *head* is now just above the water, where your board is aimed with murderous velocity.

So instead of playing Russian roulette with sections on the wave, surfers straighten off. The idea is to shift from angling to heading straight toward the beach.

The motions are *almost* identical to the ones you use for your frontside and backside turns, only less exaggerated. They depend on which way you're headed and which way you need to redirect your motion toward.

If you encounter a breaking section while surfing frontside, your escape move is a watered-down backside turn. If going backside, escape by doing a frontside straighten off. It's that simple.

To avoid a falling section while angling frontside to the right, put extra weight over your back foot, lean back a bit (to 9 o'clock) and twist around to the left. Then recenter. The nose of the board comes up a bit, the board redirects toward the beach, and, as the section falls, you remain on top of the board, traveling straight off in the whitewater.

When angling backside to the left, shift your weight to the ball and toes of your back foot, lean forward to 3 o'clock, and twist around to the right. Recenter yourself on the board and the board should be heading toward the beach.

You lefties be sure to reverse everything.

There is another, easy way to exit a section. Simply go over the top.

Over the Top

You can also avoid sections while angling on a wave by turning *in,* toward the wave while angling, thus taking you up and over the top. You exit the wave by going up over the top and out the back.

Beginners seem to have trouble remembering this while riding a wave. There's something about the human mind that causes it to overlook this easiest of escape moves while in the act of riding a surfboard. Practice going over the top by doing it when you don't have to. Just turn into the wave as you're angling along with no sections looming ahead of you. In exchange for wasting part of your ride to practice this, you'll be giving yourself the gift of being able to do it when it's necessary.

Here's how it works:

Going frontside? Do a frontside turn. Over the top and out.

Going backside? Do a backside turn. Over the top and out.

The only hitch is that you must not hesitate when it comes to exiting a wave by going over the top.

Should you delay too long in going over the top, the wave might break at the exact instant that you're up there at the very top. You'll be going over the falls. "Over the falls" is just about as bad as it sounds. You get embedded in the breaking part of the wave and crash forward and down with it and then get the hell beat out of you by it. Good way to get hit by your board, too.

She who hesitates is lost. Whatever you do, don't go taking half measures when going over the top. Do it and be done with it. Save the second thoughts for when you're sitting safely on the beach after a fun session of surfing.

Stringing Moves Together

You're just about there. With frontside and backside turns, avoidance techniques, knowledge of wave shape, and all the rest of it, you can string moves together and actually *do things* on your surfboard.

Now you can begin to articulate your surfboard. Just aim and shoot. You can do whatever your heart desires (and your increasing ability permits). You're in the freedom zone. Free to try weird new moves upon a wave. Free to just stand there, gliding across the wave, and feel the offshore wind blowing through your hair. From here on out it's up to you.

Here's a sample ride as a recap of everything you've learned:

A check of the surf at your local beach revealed nice, 3-foot waves brushed to perfection by a 10-mile-per-hour offshore breeze. You drove home, grabbed the board and all your gear, and tied the board to the roof of the car.

You applied sunscreen to your exposed skin. At the water's edge you waxed your board thoroughly. You put the wax in your pocket (if you're wearing baggies). After that you attached your leash to your ankle, picked up the board, and walked out into the waves.

Holding the board under your arm pointed nose first into the oncoming waves, you walked out to where the water was about waist deep. You laid the board down on the water with the nose still pointing out to sea and climbed up on top of it.

Paddling seaward using a crawl stroke, you held on tight as several small whitewaters washed over you. When each had passed over, you resumed paddling. Eventually you arrived out past the breakers where all the other surfers were sitting, waiting to catch the next wave.

Sitting up on your board, you spotted a set of waves stacking up out on the horizon, heading shoreward. As the set arrived, several other surfers jockeyed for position and stroked into the waves. Eyeing the waves with other surfers jostling each other for position, you wisely decided to wait it out in the hopes that another wave or two might come in after the main part of the set.

Your patience was rewarded by a nice 3-foot wave that slipped in after all the other surfers in your vicinity had taken off. The shape of the wave indicated that it would peel off to the right. This made you happy, because right is frontside for you.

As the wave approached, you pivoted the board around and began sprint paddling, butterfly-style, while the wave came under you and began lifting you. Just as you began to start back down the face of the wave, you gave three more good strokes and then leapt up into your stance. As you came to your feet, you looked down the line and verified that the wave was not going to close out.

Dropping down to the bottom of the wave, you applied a little weight to your power foot, leaned forward, and twisted around to the right. The board came around smartly and aligned itself with the wall of the wave. At this point, you recentered your weight over the middle of the board and began angling, at a high rate of speed, down the wall of the wave.

Looking ahead, you could see a section building. At the speed you were traveling, you thought you might have enough velocity to beat the section down the line.

The wave became steeper and steeper ahead of you. Your speed increased. You felt as if you were flying. As you whistled along like a rifle shot, the wave began breaking just behind you, racing along with you and urging you to go even faster if you could. As the section broke, the wave formed a lip of green crystal that flickered and danced mere

A beautifully executed frontside turn.

inches from your body. You evaded the crashing force of the wave like a matador evades the horns of the bull. The exhilaration took your breath away.

Firing down the line, you made it past the section only to see that the wave was going to close out altogether a bit farther on. As the wave drew itself up along its entire length, you weighted back on your power foot once again and leaned back a bit while twisting to the left. The board redirected from racing down the line and pointed toward the beach. When the wave broke, you were recentered over your board and heading straight in. Deciding that you'd had enough excitement for the moment, you rode the whitewater all the way to the beach and stepped off the board grinning from ear to ear.

Of course, it will be a while before your rides go as nicely as that. But at some point your hard work will be rewarded.

Bodyboarding and Bodysurfing

With a Bodyboard

A bodyboard is a very short, spongelike board on which you ride while lying on your stomach. Steering a bodyboard is such an intuitive thing that I'm sure you'll figure it out. (Hint: Just lean in the direction you want to go.)

The only thing to learn in bodyboarding is the kinds of waves you want to look for. It boils down to this: Waves you should stay off when riding a surfboard turn out to be just right for a bodyboard.

On a bodyboard, it doesn't matter if a wave is closing out. Later, when you get really good at bodyboarding, you'll want to ride waves with good shape just like stand-up surfers. But for now, you can have a blast on vicious closeouts that would put you in the hospital if you tried to ride them on a surfboard. And this extends to expert bodyboarders. Hammering along into a funneling closeout on a bodyboard is *always* fun. No matter how long you've been bodyboarding.

Booming closeouts, by the way, most often occur close to the shore, just off the beach, in the shorebreak. So you don't have to kick your flippers for half a mile to get all the way out there. Just jump into the shorebreak and have a blast. But be sure that the waves aren't coming over onto *dry* sand. You'll be picking grit out of body orifices for a week. Also be careful not to plunge *directly* head first into the shallow water out in front of a wave you're riding. The danger of hitting bottom head first is that you could break your neck.

A wave that jumps up and crashes over violently, forming a nice tube as it does so, is perfect for bodyboarding. The momentary view of the inner lining of a wave, just before it explodes, is always thrilling.

Bodyboarding is a nice complement to surfing because it allows you to use different kinds of waves, optimizing the days you can be out there in the water.

With Fins Only

You can also go the minimalist route and skip the bodyboard, riding the shorebreak with fins alone.

Bodysurfing, like bodyboarding, is best done in waves that break with extra power and vigor. Booming shorebreak is just right.

You can do a truly surprising amount of stuff using nothing more than the planing area afforded by your body. You can *angle* down the line like a rifle shot, if you work at it.

With the fins on, swim and kick like hell into a robust wave just before it breaks. As you feel yourself start to drop down and into the wave, put an arm out straight. Just one arm. The one on the side of you that you want to travel toward. Let that arm become an additional planing surface, held out in front of you, lying on the wave face. You can even flatten your hand to provide a hair more of planing surface.

Spling! and down the line you go!

Apply yourself and you can learn to do rolls and all sorts of other weird stuff.

If you fetch up in Hawaii, take a day to head out to the southeast end of Oahu to a place called Makapuu. There're guys there doing things on waves with just their bodies that you'd never believe possible. Ditto certain rare days at the Banzai Pipeline. If you're in California, go to Newport Beach when a large south swell is running. Ask around for directions to get to The Wedge. The bodysurfing carnage is truly eye-popping. *Do not* attempt to go out and try it for yourself.

And if you dislike encumbrances of any kind, take the fins off. You can *still* bodysurf—just not as efficiently. Hell, for that matter, go ahead and leave the swimsuit on the beach. Bodysurfing works quite well with nothing at all except your own self.

Surfing Etiquette

There are rules of surfing etiquette. Keep the following points in mind. You don't want to get crosswise with the local crew.

In general, it works this way:

1) People coming your way who are closer to the breaking part of the wave have the right-of-way. In other words, *do not* take off on a wave in front of anybody angling in your direction. They got it first, it's theirs. Period.

2) No whining. No moaning. No complaints. If you don't like the intensity of the crowd that's snatching every last wave before you have a chance to paddle for it, then go somewhere else.

   An integral part of surfing is working your way up the pecking order far enough to get a reasonable number of waves when you go out.

   Don't even think about jumping line in the pecking order. The *only* thing that matters out in the *lineup* (that's where the waves break) is surfing ability. All else remains on the beach. That includes bank accounts, college degrees, famous relatives, political connections, shiny cars, *everything.*

   Out in the water it's the strictest of strict meritocracies.

3) In the world of surfing there's a hierarchy of surfspots as well as surfing ability. The best surfers surf at the best surfspots. And the competition for waves is cutthroat.

   As a beginner, always pick a surfspot that's not so far up there on the food chain. You'll know in a hurry if you've chosen the wrong place to surf. You'll be able to slice the intimidation with a knife. Go somewhere else until you get good at surfing. Less hassle.

4) If you're paddling out, the guy on the wave has the right-of-way. What this means is that it's up to you, as a paddler, to get the hell out of the way of anybody up and riding on a wave. Practically speaking, if while you're paddling out you encounter someone up and riding on a wave coming

your way, you're often forced to go paddle through the whitewater instead of being able to paddle around the whitewater, on the unbroken part of the wave. That's where the person who you're supposed to get out of the way of is surfing. Don't ruin her ride by selfishly paddling right in front of her. Besides, she might just run right over you. Happens all the time.

5) Keep in mind that all matters of surfing etiquette are subject to the size and attitude of whomever you're dealing with. Miss Manners can't surf, isn't out there with you, and wouldn't be listened to for half a second even if she were.

Remember, it's the real world out there. And these are real people. And the cops are stuck way back up on the beach along with everybody else who can't come out into the waves with you. Mind yourself.

6) *One lousy beer can* on the sand is more than we want to put up with. Cigarette butts, too. Glass containers inevitably break sooner or later. Chances are that somebody's perfectly innocent and well-behaved five-year-old will slice her foot.

The above admonition is not given for no reason. Surfers are among the more environmentally aware. They care. They're also unruly, well muscled, and impulsive. I've seen people who were *made* to clean up the trash they attempted to leave on the beach by surfers.

Clean the place up when you leave.

Tar, of course, is a different matter. If you've got tar on your beach, it comes from the bilges of ships nearby that are pumping it overboard with the bilgewater, or from an oil spill. Watch out for tar. If it gets on your surfboard, it's going to get all over you, too. Check the bottoms of your feet just before you walk out into the water. If there's tar, use a shell or something to scrape off the thickest globs of it, and use liquid cooking oil on a paper towel to wipe away the rest of it.

Waves, Wind, and Tide

Reading Waves

This is something I've touched upon several times already. But it's worth a bit more attention.

You want to learn how to tell what a wave's going to do before it does it. The ability to anticipate a wave will do wonders for your ability as a surfer. It'll allow you to successfully predict *when* a wave's going to break, *where* it'll break, *how hard* it'll break, and how all that and more relates to your next move on your surfboard.

What you're trying to do is to tell by the way a wave looks how it'll act. People who don't surf can't look at waves this way. So you really can't start seriously reading waves until you've surfed enough to have some sense about where you'd like to be going on a wave and what you'd like to be doing when you get there. Here are a few tips to keep in mind:

⊃ The shape of waves is affected by the bottom profile of the ocean floor, reef, sandbar, or what have you that the wave is traveling across.

⊃ Shallow water causes waves to break; deep water causes them to *back off,* or go from whitewater back to rollers.

⊃ Larger waves break in deeper water—all other things being equal—than smaller waves.

⊃ When two waves combine, they produce one wave that's bigger and more powerful than either of the original two.

⊃ The direction a wave travels can have a strong effect on whether, or how, it'll hit various deep and shallow areas, and thus whether and how it'll break.

When you're down at the beach spending time out of the water, keep your eyes on the waves to see what they do, where they do it, and how they do it, and try to figure out *why* they're doing what they're doing. It isn't as complicated as it sounds.

Especially if there're other people out there surfing. Watch how the varying aspects of the waves affect the surfing that's going on.

With time, you'll get to the point where you can come down to a beach you've never seen before and amaze your friends and family by telling them where the deep water is and all sorts of other arcana. Helps with the surfing, too.

Tide

The tide is what everybody who doesn't surf thinks makes the waves. They're wrong. Wind makes waves. Tide makes . . . life difficult. The tide is sneaky. It moves like the hour hand on your watch. You never see it move, but it moves anyway.

The tide, by altering the depth of the water, can have radical effects upon the waves breaking at a given beach.

Some areas, such as the Gulf Coast, have very minimal tides that have near-zero effect on the waves. When learning to surf, you may ignore the tides at places like this. Other places are not so forgiving.

Waves that were easy crumblers four hours ago when you last looked at them can turn into karate-chopping shorebreak that'll hurt you if you attempt to ride it. And vice versa.

Keep an eye on the tides and don't be fooled.

Later, when you start to get good at reading waves and understanding the effects of the tide, you'll be able to successfully predict surf conditions based on what the tide will be doing.

Wind

Wind has been discussed before, but it deserves to be looked at in greater detail. You already know what offshore and onshore winds are.

Generally speaking, offshore winds are your friend. Onshore winds are evil. Onshores, while having the ability to at least produce waves, will take otherwise perfectly good surf and ruin it. Onshore breezes cause the ocean to take on a choppy, crinkled appearance that messes up the surfing. All that chop and crinkle makes for lousy rides, like skateboarding on a gravel road rather than nice smooth concrete. The stronger the onshore wind, the worse the surf. At 2 to 3 miles an hour, an onshore breeze is no big deal. But at 10 to 15 miles per hour, things go down the toilet in a hurry.

That choppiness also causes the waves to break here, there, and wherever else they might take a notion to, without a discernible pattern, and then back off, making it impossible for you to stay on the wave without a damn outboard motor.

Unless they're howling (happens all the time in Hawaii), offshore winds make for tip-top surfing. The effect they have of brushing the waves to a pristine state is just what the doctor ordered.

But on the eastern seaboard of the United States, offshore winds have a sinister secret weapon. They kill waves. East Coast swells are often generated by whatever strong onshore wind happens to be blowing at the time. Choppy waves. As soon as the onshore stops and the offshores kick in, the waves get really good—but they get blown down to nothingness in short order. No more onshore to generate the waves, no more waves. This is an effect of geography coupled with the global circulation patterns of the atmosphere and there's not a thing you can do about it. (Except move, like I did.)

Hawaii and California have it better. By virtue of extraordinarily fortunate geographical placement, both of those coasts are favored with prevailing offshore winds over the very areas that are exposed to swell after swell after swell. What it means is that the wind can blow offshore for all it's worth and the waves just keep on coming.

Unless you're in Hawaii, where the trade wind blows the same way for . . . oh, say 350 days out of the year, you'll want to become familiar with those times when an offshore wind is likely to blow.

That's usually in the morning and that's when you want to be hitting the surf. Dawn patrol. That's why so many surfers have second shift jobs.

At night, land cools off more than the ocean. Air settles over the land and then eases out over the ocean, where it rises. This is called a land breeze. It's the opposite of a sea breeze, which kicks in with onshores in the afternoon because the land has heated up more than the ocean, causing the whole process to reverse itself. Meteorology 101.

Speaking of which, be sure to keep an eye on the Weather Channel as often as you can. Those guys are going to be telling you all sorts of good stuff. Not deliberately, though. As a wholly accidental side effect of giving the farmers in Iowa and the skiers in Utah their latest update on what's coming, they also tell the surfers a whole lot about waves that are on the way. You might even learn how to read isobar maps, which tell you all you need to know about wind speed and direction. Wind speed and direction create waves out in the middle of the ocean and then determine if those waves are going to be choppy or smooth locally where you surf.

Knowing Your Limits

Finally, know when to say when. Know when to stay out of the water. Don't try to impress anybody by paddling out on a day when the ocean is in a foul mood and has blood in its eye.

Know your limits. How long can you get thrashed around underwater in a nightmare wipeout and successfully hold your breath? Don't exceed this time limit. Penalty: death. No right of appeal. Sentence to be carried out immediately.

We're not fooling around here, folks. Watch it.

Never surf farther from the beach than you can reasonably expect to swim—through pounding surf—if your cord breaks and the board is carried all the way to the beach. Don't exceed this distance limit.

A beginner has no business in surf like this.

Surfing opens up a whole new universe. A universe filled with thrills and excitement like you've never seen before. Once you've mastered the basics, surfing invites you to explore exotic new waves and maneuvers in a never-ending progression. It's more fun than you can imagine. It's a lifetime of people, places, and events that will never cease to amaze and elate you.

Come on in, the water's fine.

Confessional Glossary

I have a confession to make. I've deliberately
misled you. I intentionally called things by names
that most surfers don't use. But I did it for a
reason. To avoid choking you on lingo.

So here's a limited glossary of some of the terms that the people you're going to be meeting down at the beach will be using. This list is by no means exhaustive. Surfing lingo is a surprisingly rich and ramified subset of the English language. Parts of it have entered the world of standard usage. Who doesn't know what a *wipeout* is? That and other terms are used by nonsurfers every day without their knowing the origins of the terms they use. Surfing lingo evolves and changes with each passing year. If you want to talk with surfers, you've got to learn the lingo.

BACK OFF, BACKOFF: 1) When a wave dies down by encountering deep water. Often a wave completely, sometimes partially, reverts from foaming whitewater to smooth roller. 2) The deep water where this happens. Waves don't die out in the trough, they back off in the backoff.

BACKSIDE: Surfing down the *line*, in *trim*, with your body facing away from the wave.

BAGGIES: Surf trunks. Made especially for surfing by specialty clothing outfits. Don't put a sandwich in your baggies. Put yourself in 'em instead.

BEACHBREAK: 1) A sand-bottom place with no particular geographical peculiarities. Just a straight sand beach without any frills or special effects. This is where you want to go to learn to surf. 2) The type of wave that breaks at a beachbreak.

BLANK: 1) The polyurethane core of a surfboard before it gets shaped. 2) The look on most people's faces when you talk surf lingo at them.

BODYBOARD: A sawed-off little surfboard, about 4 feet long, that you ride lying down upon. Made from soft spongelike material. Very safe, with excellent handling characteristics. Likes to be ridden in pounding *shorebreak*, though; be careful.

BODYBOARDING, BELLYBOARDING: Surfing while lying down on a *bodyboard* instead of standing up on a surfboard.

BODYSURFING: Surfing without benefit of anything except your own body, and maybe a pair of *fins*.

CHOPPY: The ocean under an *onshore wind*. Covered with short, disorganized waves coming every which way. Lousy for surfing.

CLEAN: The absence of *chop* or other disorganization on a wave. The sort of conditions you look for when surfing.

CLEANUP SET: A set of especially large waves. Rogue waves. A cleanup set will break farther out in the ocean than where you're sitting in the *lineup* and give you a good thrashing. Sunset Beach is notorious for its cleanup sets.

CLOSEOUT: When a long wall of a wave all breaks at the same time. Poor for surfing, unless you haven't learned how to *trim* yet.

CORD: Shock-absorbent *leash* that attaches your ankle to your surfboard.

CUTBACK: A turn wherein you reverse your direction completely, right to left or left to right. You may do a *frontside* cutback or a *backside* cutback to change your direction.

DECK: The upper surface of your surfboard. The part you stand on.

DING: Damage to a surfboard. Or other things, too. If your board washes up on some rocks, it's likely to get dinged.

DOUBLE UP: When one wave overtakes another. Results in a momentary dramatic increase in wave power.

DROP, TAKE THE DROP: Take off on a wave.

DROP IN: 1) Catch a wave. 2) Steal a wave from someone by taking off in front of her after she's already up and riding. Excellent fight starter. Don't do it.

FACE: The smooth, unbroken portion of the wave. The part you ride.

FADE: To take off or travel in one direction (counter to what the *shape* of the wave dictates) prior to carving a nice turn the other way.

FEATHER, FEATHERING: The effect of *offshore wind* blowing spray off the top of a steep wave just before it breaks.

FIN, OR FINS: The fin at the tail of your surfboard that projects down and into the water to provide steering stability. Used to be called a skeg in the old days, but if you use the word now, people will look at you funny. Some surfboards have more than one fin. You only need one for now. Save the multifin boards till your surfing improves. The fewer sharp edges to cleave your hide with, the better.

FINS: Flippers for your feet, especially designed for *bodyboarding* or *bodysurfing*, that help you kick along and ride waves.

FLOATER: Momentarily surfing on the outer, top portion of the *lip* before falling down and in front of the wave while it breaks and continuing your ride. Difficult maneuver.

FOAM: The polyurethane core of a surfboard.

FRONTSIDE: Surfing down the *line*, in *trim*, with your body facing the wave.

GLASS, GLASS JOB: The resin-impregnated, fiberglass outer skin of a surfboard.

GLASSY: Surf with either light *offshore wind* or no wind at all. Looks like glass. Nice for surfing.

GOOFY FOOT, GOOFY FOOTER: Surfers who surf with their right foot forward, left foot back. Goofy foot surfers surf *frontside* on *lefts* and are usually left-handed people.

HANG TEN: The business of running all the way up to the extreme front end of your *longboard* (physics prevents this trick from being done on a *shortboard*) and placing the toes of both feet over the front edge of the board while you ride a wave. Amazingly difficult move. The term is often used incorrectly by the media; none of those people know what "hang ten" really means, and they always use it in conjunction with pictures of guys on *shortboards,* tearing radical *cutbacks,* getting *tubed,* or anything else except actually hanging ten. Good laugh-getter for people who really surf.

HITTING THE LIP: A move wherein a surfer turns hard from the bottom of the wave, goes up to the top, making solid contact with the *lip* as it breaks, and then rebounds down the wave in a sharp, snapping turn.

HOLLOW: Especially open-*tubed.*

INSIDE: Toward the shore. The area of breaking waves that's closest to the beach.

KICKOUT: Finishing up a ride by "kicking" the board over the top of the wave in a tight turning maneuver.

KOOK: A lousy surfer. A beginner. You.

LEASH: *Cord.*

LEFT: 1) Toward the left as you're facing the beach, paddling for a wave. 2) A wave that breaks or peels off in this direction. Pipeline is a famous left.

LIFT: Forces generated on your surfboard that hold you up.

LINEUP, LINE UP: 1) The particular location where a wave breaks. The generalized area where everybody sits waiting for the next wave. 2) Align landmarks on the near shore with landmarks in the far distance, to provide a proper navigational fix on your exact whereabouts in the water despite the best efforts of currents, waves, and pushy *locals* to cause you to drift elsewhere.

LINES: Swells coming from far away in the form of waves that extend sometimes for miles as long, even walls of water. Nice for surfing unless they're *closing out.*

LIP: The breaking portion of a *tubing* wave that *pitches out* and down in front of the main body of the wave. Will knock you silly if it hits you.

LOCAL, LOCALS: The people who live nearby and surf a given *surfspot* day after day after day. Can become quite agitated at the sight of a new face in the *lineup.* Treat them with respect.

LONGBOARD: A surfboard over 8 feet in length. What you want to be learning on. But be sure to get one at least 9 feet long.

LULL: A period of time wherein waves either quit coming altogether or arrive at a much reduced size. A break in the action between *sets.* Paddle out through the breakers when there's a lull. When checking the surf, be sure to watch long enough to verify that what you're seeing isn't a lull. Even on very large days, during a lull the waves may appear quite small and safe.

MUSH: Waves that break softly or sloppily with little power. You want to learn on mush. It's a lot safer.

NOSE: The front end of your surfboard.

OFFSHORE, OFFSHORE WIND: A breeze that blows out to the surf—off the shore and toward the ocean. Good for surfing.

ONSHORE, ONSHORE WIND: A breeze that blows in from the surf—onto the shore from the ocean. Lousy for surfing.

OUTSIDE: Toward the horizon. That area of breaking waves that's farthest from the beach.

OVERHEAD: Waves that exceed the height of the rider. Overhead waves are difficult to paddle out through.

OVER THE FALLS: To become entrained within the breaking portion of a wave and get the hell beat out of you as the wave breaks.

PEAK: A wave that has a distinctively humped-up appearance, with a tall part in the middle sloping off to either side. Peaks are really good waves at *beachbreaks*.

Always pay attention to what's coming your way from outside.

PEARL: The *nose* of the board catches and dips below the water, bringing your ride to an abrupt end with you flung into the water gracelessly.

PEEL OFF: The process whereby a wave breaks starting off in one particular place and then zippering along cleanly and evenly for a distance. The opposite of a *closeout*.

PITCHING OUT: Breaking (as in a wave) with extra thrust and vigor. Forming a *lip* that travels farther out in front of the main body of the wave than usual. Great for experts, hell on beginners.

POINTBREAK: 1) A *surfspot* where waves encounter a bend in the coastline, causing them to *peel off* with machinelike precision. 2) The wave that breaks at a pointbreak. Very nice. Always very crowded. Go someplace else.

RAIL: The side of your surfboard. You don't carry a surfboard under your arm by grabbing the far side of it with your hand, you grab the rail.

REEFBREAK: 1) A *surfspot* where waves encounter a distinctively contoured reef, causing them to break with distinctively good *shape.* 2) A wave that breaks at a reefbreak.

REGULAR FOOT: Surfers who surf with their left foot forward. Regular foot surfers surf *frontside* on *rights,* and are generally right-handed.

RIGHT: 1) Toward the right as you're facing the beach, paddling for a wave. 2) A wave that breaks or *peels off* in this direction. Malibu is a famous right.

SECTION: 1) A piece of *closeout.* Any part of a wave that breaks out of sequence, forming an area of *soup* ahead of you that's going to spoil your ride. If you're good, you can anticipate sections and drive like hell down the *line* to outrace them. 2) Any distinctive part of an otherwise well-shaped wave. The *inside* section at Sunset Beach will give you the *tube ride* of your life if it doesn't kill you instead.

SET: A series of waves, one right after another. Most sets have anywhere from three to six waves, but they can occasionally contain dozens. Don't attempt to paddle out through the breakers when a set is pouring through. Wait for the *lull.*

SHAPE: 1) The characteristic way that a wave breaks. Waves can have good shape or bad shape. 2) The particular design of a given surfboard. 3) The act of creating a surfboard by shaping it from a foam *blank.*

SHOOTING THE CURL: Something you should never, ever say, unless you want to be regarded as a hopeless dork whose entire education on things surfish consists of having watched Hollywood trash movies containing surfing as either the main subject or a mere side issue. Hollywood gets it wrong every single time.

SHOREBREAK: The last little bit where the waves re-form out of the *backoff* and break nearly right on the shore. Waves usually break with extra violence in the shorebreak. Be careful.

SHOREPOUND: The *shorebreak.*

SHORTBOARD: A surfboard usually around 6 feet in length. Avoid using one till you get good at surfing.

SHOULDER: The part of the wave that slopes away from the breaking portion. This is what you want to head toward after you catch a wave. *Peaks* have a shoulder on both sides. *Pointbreak* waves only have one shoulder, on one side, and some rocks or something on the other. *Closeouts* have no shoulder at all.

SIDESHORE: A breeze blowing parallel to the beach. Not really *onshore.* Not really *offshore.* Not really very good for surfing either.

SINGLE FIN: A surfboard with a single *fin.*

SLOP: Lousy surf. Weak surf. Lousy weak surf. Good for learning in but pretty much worthless after you've mastered the basics.

SNAPBACK, SNAP: A *cutback.* Done maybe a little faster.

SOFTBOARD: A surfboard made from a spongelike material that's much safer to be hit with when learning but also has horrid handling characteristics that can stunt your surfing growth.

SOUP: Whitewater. Never say "whitewater." Always say "soup." If you don't, all the other surfers will think you're from Mars or something. You don't ride the whitewater. You ride the soup.

SPINOUT: To have the *fin(s)* of your board come out of the wave, resulting in the board jumping or falling suddenly sideways and causing a *wipeout*.

SPIT: A gust of mist and water droplets that's ejected from within the *tube* of particularly hard-breaking, *hollow* waves. An uncanny apparition not seen in most waves.

SPONGE: A *bodyboard*.

SPONGER, SPONGE RIDER: The person who rides a *bodyboard*.

STALL: To lose lift and speed, causing you to lose the wave. Also to deliberately stall momentarily in order to better place yourself on a wave.

STRAIGHT OFF: Surfing directly toward the beach, as opposed to angling down the line to the *left* or the *right*.

STRINGER: The thin central, longitudinal, structural element of a surfboard installed to give the board added strength. Usually made of wood.

SURFSPOT: A particular geographical location for riding waves.

SURFWAX: *Wax*.

TAIL: The rear end of your surfboard.

THRUSTER: A surfboard with a three-fin, or tri-fin, setup.

TRACTION PAD: Recycled Michelins glued to the *deck* of your surfboard to give you extra grip and traction.

TRIMMING, TRIM: Riding the board at an angle to the wave, sidelong down the length of the beach, instead of aiming straight at the beach as you ride; also the condition wherein the board is doing so. If you ever say "angle" when you're down at the beach, nobody will understand you. They quit saying "angle" back around the late '50s. Too bad; it was a good descriptive word.

TUBE: 1) The hole formed in the water when a wave breaks by plunging over vigorously instead of just crumbling weakly. 2) Any wave that forms a tube when breaking. Excellent surf for adepts, rough on beginners.

TUBE RIDE, TUBED: The business of riding along inside the *tube* produced by a powerful, well-shaped wave. Exquisitely enjoyable. Lasts just a second or three, usually. More addictive than heroin. Possibly more dangerous, too. Waves *tube* as a result of abruptly encountering very shallow water. Tube riding is perhaps the most pleasurable aspect of surfing but it's dangerous as hell, too. If you *wipeout* while getting tubed, you stand a good chance of hitting the bottom quite hard.

VICTORY AT SEA: Large, choppy surf. Go have a look at the opening credits of the old '50s TV show about World War II naval engagements.

WAX: *Surfwax* you apply to the upper surface of your surfboard to provide necessary grip and traction. Don't leave it in the pocket of your *baggies* when you launder them.

WIPEOUT: To fall off, or get knocked off, your surfboard. Also the fall itself. "He took a wipeout." Or, "He had a bad wipeout."

Index